MUSIC
BOXES

MUSIC BOXES

THE COLLECTOR'S GUIDE TO SELECTING, RESTORING,
AND ENJOYING NEW AND VINTAGE MUSIC BOXES

Gilbert Bahl

COURAGE BOOKS

An Imprint of
RUNNING PRESS
Philadelphia, Pennsylvania

A QUINTET BOOK

Canadian Representatives:
General Publishing Co., Ltd.
30 Lesmill Road, Don Mills
Ontario M3B 2T6

9 8 7 6 5 4 3 2 1
Digit on the right indicates the number of this printing

Library of Congress
Cataloging-in-Publication Number 93-70598

ISBN 1-56138-220-5

This book was designed and produced by
Quintet Publishing Limited
6 Blundell Street
London N7 9BH

Creative Director: Richard Dewing
Designer: Ian Hunt
Project Editor: Helen Denholm
Editor: Lydia Darbyshire
Photographer: Harry Rinker

Typeset in Great Britain by
Central Southern Typesetters, Eastbourne
Manufactured in Hong Kong by
Regent Publishing Services Limited
Printed in Hong Kong by
Leefung-Asco Printers Limited

PICTURE CREDITS

With grateful thanks to Keith Harding for the loan of
the photographs on page 12 and page 13 (top) and to
Heber Sell for loaning items for photography.

Published by Courage Books
an imprint of Running Press Book Publishers
125 South Twenty-second Street
Philadelphia, Pennsylvania 19103–4399

CONTENTS

INTRODUCTION

Music boxes are enchanting, magical, nostalgic, and exciting, appealing to people of all ages. Play a music box in a room full of people, and they will stop to listen. You will find that music boxes never fail to captivate and enchant and that collecting them is an enjoyable and fascinating hobby.

Your interest in music boxes may have been stimulated by the sounds that they produce; or you may have been fascinated by the rise and fall of the teeth as the cylinder turns. You may have been given a music box as a gift or, if you are fortunate, you may have inherited a treasured family heirloom. You may have a special interest in music boxes that combine novelty features with the musical movement. The early automata that combine the most exquisitely fashioned figures with music boxes are rare and eagerly sought after by collectors, but many 19th-century makers combined bells and drums or moving figures with different musical mechanisms, and several modern companies produce a variety of unusual and entertaining music boxes.

An undeniable part of the charm of an antique music box is the link it offers us with earlier times. When we hear the notes from an old and cared for box, we know that these same sounds were heard by the first owners of that box. There is also the fact that, despite the array of electronic gadgetry that surrounds us today, the workmanship and quality of these pieces can still astonish and delight us.

The term music box embraces a far wider range of objects than the cylinder boxes that were so widely produced in Switzerland and Germany in the 19th century. These boxes are, of course, keenly collected, but today's collector is as likely to be interested in disc music boxes, which were made in

LEFT **An elegant baroque table-top case, dating from c.1975, houses a new 11in (28cm) Thorens disc player, with a disc in playing position.**

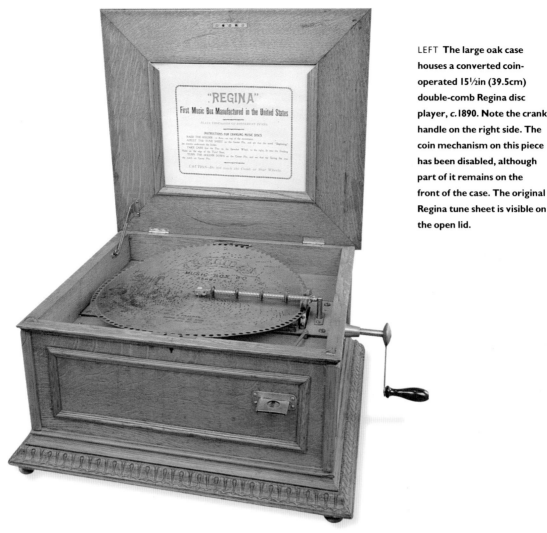

"REGINA"

First Music Box Manufactured in the United States

LEFT **The large oak case houses a converted coin-operated 15½in (39.5cm) double-comb Regina disc player, *c.*1890. Note the crank handle on the right side. The coin mechanism on this piece has been disabled, although part of it remains on the front of the case. The original Regina tune sheet is visible on the open lid.**

great quantity in both Europe and the United States in the last decades of the 19th century. These disc music boxes were a popular source of home entertainment in the days before phonographs, and some were even coin-operated – the precursors of the juke box.

The Musical Box Society International defines the term music box as:

> a popular term covering all types of automatically played musical machines, from small table-top instruments that use a cylinder or disc to play tunes on a steel comb, to large orchestrions [and] carousel organs, which have the musical capability of a symphony orchestra or a military band. Between these extremes are dozens of mechanical music-makers, including

reproducing pianos, automatic violin-playing machines, clocks with musical attachments, musical toys and novelties, the familiar player piano, and many more.

It may, in fact, be easier to say what should not be included in the category. The term music box is not used to describe a system that plays back pre-recorded music – by a tape-recorder, for example – nor music that is non-mechanical – computer-generated sounds, for example. Both these types of music require electronic speakers and amplification systems, and they are not included in the discussion that follows.

The two main types of music box discussed in this book are based on two different types of music-making unit – the cylinder and the disc.

ABOVE **Many collectors regard Regina disc music boxes as the finest ever made. The good cabinet construction, for which the company was renowned, can be seen in this view of a large floor-standing model. This has a piano-type sound board, which gave good resonance.**

Acquiring a good quality music box is not beyond the price range of most people. Decorated cases were provided for the better quality mechanisms, and a few cases, which may have been made to special order, are so elaborately and exquisitely made and decorated that they are in a class of their own. Some of the earlier cylinder boxes that play several tunes are undeniably expensive. An interchangeable cylinder music box, made by Nicole Frères and playing 36 airs on six cylinders, each 13in (33cm) long, for example, sold at auction in London in 1989 for more than $6,000 (£3,800). However, many of the cases were plain and some versions were produced in large quantities, and it is still possible to find desirable and collectable examples. Music boxes should not be used as a means of financial investment. Most good quality boxes do, in fact, appreciate in value over time, but trying to plan and manage their acquisition and expecting a good financial return is neither reasonable nor practicable.

Most collectors find that acquiring one or two fine examples is a satisfying and pleasurable experience. The pieces you acquire may well become treasured family heirlooms, but in the meantime you will have had the enjoyment and pride in possessing a work of art that both looks and sounds beautiful.

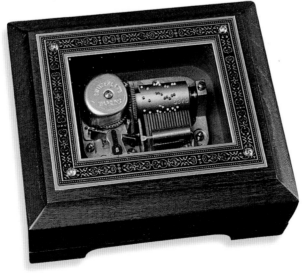

RIGHT **This modern cherry case houses a single-tune, 18-note (1/18) Thorens movement, which may be seen through the fixed lens. The piece, which was made in the 1980s, is wound from the bottom, and the on/off control is activated by tilting the box to the right to start it and tilting it to the left to** stop it. **This model was available playing a range of popular tunes, including "Edelweiss", "Lara's Theme", "Memory" (from** Cats**), and "Für Elise", while more recent versions play "Wind Beneath My Wings" and selections from** Phantom of the Opera**.**

THE · CYLINDER MUSIC BOX

CHAPTER

I

The barrel organ was one of the first means of reproducing music mechanically, and some fine specimens were made in the early 16th century. The cylinder music box, however, was the first form of musical instrument that was small enough to allow people to enjoy music in their own homes without playing an instrument themselves.

The music box is actually based on a very simple principle: metal teeth which are tuned to scale in a variety of ways are plucked by pins projecting from a revolving cylinder. These pins are set in the cylinder in such a way that they pluck the teeth of the comb at precisely the right moment. Although the shape and size of music boxes have changed over the years, the same basic system has continued to be used.

The first simple musical movements were found in watches made in Switzerland. In the 16th century the notes were produced by a revolving disc with teeth around the edge, and the same system

LEFT AND ABOVE **This pocket watch by Reuge, c.1980, has a 2/35 movement – that is, a two-tune, 35-note movement. The 17-jewel watch and the key-wound musical movement are in a gold case. The movement has 35 hand-tuned teeth and a gilt cylinder ⅓in (8mm) in diameter. The hand-pinned cylinder has a total of 218 pins. Each tune plays for 18 seconds. Two control buttons enable the music to be played and the tune to be changed.**

continued to be used in watches and clocks made in the 18th century. The separation of the musical part of the clock from the time-keeping part did not occur until the early 19th century, when improvements to the revolving cylinder were made, although a simplified version had been used to operate hammers striking the bells in musical clocks in the late 18th century.

The invention of the first music box proper in 1796 is credited to Antoine Favre (1767–1828), a Swiss watchmaker. The musical movement involved a tuned tooth, which, in the earliest examples, was plucked either by pins set in a flat wheel or by projections in the outer surface of a spring barrel. More recently it has been suggested that the tuned tooth was not, in fact, Favre's invention, but had been in use for perhaps as long as 50 years when Favre perfected the miniature musical movement for use in his watches and snuff-boxes, and that, while Favre's was the first documented use of the tuned tooth, it may perhaps not have been the first. There seems no doubt, however, that Favre was the first person to make this mechanism small enough to be used in watches.

In 1802 a new version of the tooth and pin arrangement was introduced. This used a flat rotating disc with pins, which allowed more teeth to be used and at the same time could be housed in an even smaller case. Musical movements using this disc and pin arrangement were soon being put in items such as cane tops, bottles, seals, and snuff-boxes. In fact, so popular were musical snuff-boxes that music boxes came to be called *tabatières* (snuff-boxes.)

At first the production of the cylinder box was basically a cottage industry, with many of the parts being made or assembled at home. These parts were then sold on to others, who assembled the musical movements or made the boxes in which the movements were inserted. From about 1810 Geneva

became the center of production of a range of wonderful creations including ornate music boxes, musical pendants, perfume bottles, rings, bracelets, and watches, and mechanical lyres and harps, all of which were made of gold and adorned with enamel work and precious stones. Sainte-Croix was also a center of production and it was here that Charles Paillard set up his factory in 1875. It was this development that signalled the start of mass production of music boxes.

Early versions of the music box were usually driven by clockwork, although they sometimes required hand-turning. Their popularity led to all kinds of improvements. Soon the rotating platform or disc was replaced with a special cylinder that was placed parallel to the teeth. The way the teeth were arranged also changed. Instead of a series of individual teeth, sets of teeth arranged in groups of

ABOVE AND BELOW A mahogany case with a large cartel movement, *c.*1880, of Swiss origin, maker unknown. This is a 12-tune movement with 62 teeth.

The lid is decorated with an inlaid floral design. The outer, molded edge extends slightly over the sides of the box, and it is shaped and finished in high-gloss black.

four or five in sections, with each section made from a single piece of metal, started to be used. By around 1820 individual sections were being replaced by one comb made of a single piece of steel, which increased the resonance of the sound.

The next advance, which occurred in the early 1830s, was the introduction of the cartel box. In this, the spring arbor is mounted horizontally to the bedplate, in the same way as the cylinder. Before this, the smaller cylinder boxes were constructed so that the spring winding arbor was vertical to the bedplate.

Next came the development of longer and wider cylinders that could accommodate more pins, making it possible to play longer and more complicated tunes. Other improvements included the introduction of dampers, which were designed to prevent the teeth from vibrating excessively, which was vital if the same tooth was to be struck again almost immediately. Nicole Frères of Geneva, one of the leading makers, devised the two-comb box, which permitted variations in the intensity of the sound. This was quickly followed by the use of as many as five combs to give special effects. Cylinders almost 24in (61cm) long began to appear.

Favre described his invention as a carillon without bells. He might have regarded the trend that developed in the 1840s as a retrograde step, for at this time the inclusion of bells and drums became popular. At first these were hidden under the bedplate, but it quickly became fashionable to place them where they could be seen, at the back of the cylinder.

Reduction gears were developed to lengthen the playing time. Placing a wheel (gear) between the spring drive and the cylinder had the effect of increasing the playing time by allowing the cylinder to turn at the normal speed although the spring unwound more slowly, thus reducing the need for the mechanism to be frequently rewound. Methods of automatically setting the pins in the cylinders had already been devised, and the interchangeable cylinder which dates from 1850 meant that the repertoire could be still further augmented. These cylinders could be easily removed from the box and other cylinders, with different tunes on, could be put in instead – as long as they were designed for that particular box. In 1875 what might be called the first "long-player", which was able to provide a program lasting for three hours, was made. Some boxes had

LEFT AND BELOW **Made in the 1990s, this walnut case houses a two-tune, 50-note (2/ 50) Sankyo movement. The inside of the lid is lined with felt, and the mechanism is** **protected in a fixed lens. The unit is key-wound from the bottom, and the mechanism is activated by the button mounted in the center of the front panel.**

cylinders with larger diameters, which allowed longer tunes, or even two or three tunes, to be played in one complete revolution of the cylinder; Nicole Frères made a number of these "two tunes a turn" music boxes.

There was also a certain amount of standardization in the use of exterior controls – the winding key, the tune changer, the start/stop mechanism, and the instant stop switch – and these were increasingly placed on the lower left-hand side of the boxes. The interior controls, including the winding key or lever and the tune changer, were located inside the box so that they could be operated when the lid was raised. As the internal mechanisms became increasingly complex, it became usual to include glass shades. The glass lids were used not only to protect the mechanisms from dirt, dust, and prying fingers, but also to reduce the amount of machinery noise from the mechanism that could be heard when the tune was being played.

From 1860 it became more usual to mount music boxes in items that had practical and functional uses, and over time musical movements were increasingly housed in larger cases with veneered and ornate finishes. The design of the boxes also

changed. Instead of the lid being the same size as the box, it became usual for the lid to be slightly larger than the box so that it extended a little all round. This edge was contoured and rounded, before being finished in a high-gloss black.

In early 1875 Charles Paillard was among the Swiss manufacturers who began to use factory production. Methods evolved for reproducing cylinders using machines which lowered the cost of production dramatically. This move was made in response to competition from French makers.

The bedplate is the foundation plate that holds the other components of the movement – the spring barrel, the motor governor assembly, the cylinder assembly and so on. All the early boxes had brass bedplates, which were cast and then polished smooth. From 1873 cast iron was used by Paillard and Mermod, although makers such as Nicole Frères, Bremond and Lecoultre continued to use brass for several years, and miniature mechanisms for inclusion in snuff-boxes and the like were made of brass until zinc alloy became available. The cast iron bedplates had a ribbed surface which required little finishing, although most were given a coat of gold- or silver-colored paint.

RIGHT **A large and spectacular box from Paillard of Sainte-Croix which plays 12 tunes on a 20in (51cm) cylinder. Between the combs are 30 levers operating a reed organ and a pipe organ, which provides the sound of a singing bird. This burr walnut box is said to have been a present from Queen Victoria to a maharajah.**

ABOVE **An unusual music box with a writing slope front by Charles Ullman, Auberson, Switzerland,** *c.*1890. **There are three dancing dolls behind the musical movement.**

Upright, table, and floor-standing models were also made, and some of the larger models were used in commercial establishments. Coin-operated cylinder boxes, for example, were often placed in railroad stations.

RIGHT **A four-tune, 50-note (4/50) Reuge movement housed in a walnut case. You can see the four tunes listed inside the lid.**

CYLINDER BOX MODIFICATIONS

Over the years, modifications, additions and improvements were made to the basic cylinder box. The chief of these are listed below.

DRUM AND BELLS These novelty features, which Graham Webb describes as a "doubtful improvement," can be found on many boxes, and they were used to accent the rhythm of the tune being played.

In the earliest machines the bells were hidden at the base of the case – perhaps so that a new owner could play his music box and puzzle his friends about the source of the strange noise. The first drum and bell mechanisms were undeniably crude. Music boxes with concealed bells are deeper than normal, and they are often housed in beautifully made cases. They were made by many manufacturers, and have even been found hidden in music boxes with forte-piano movements.

As the feature became more popular, the bells and drum were brought into view, possibly to add an extra dimension to the entertainment on offer. The bell hammers were then made in ornamental shapes, sometimes surmounted by metal birds or butterflies, and some bells had designs engraved upon them or were decorated in brightly colored enamel paints.

ABOVE **This antique cylinder music box (c.1886, maker unknown) is housed in an extra-deep case. In addition** **to the cylinder movement, there are a set of bells with bee strikers and a drum. The bedplate mounting hardware** **is visible about half-way up the front of the case. The depth of the box and the high mounting of the movement** **allows the mechanism that operates the drum and bell to be fitted in the bottom of the case.**

The drums became miniature versions of the real thing, with parchment heads and brass wire snares.

When tuned bells were used to enhance the melody, the result was often pleasing. However, it has been suggested that during the declining years of the large cylinder box, these features, together with glass lids, were used to help disguise the noises made by the playing mechanism. It was also found that bells could be used to cover up a poor tone or lackadaisical arrangement, and by the 1890s some 6in (15cm) cylinders and three bells were making remarkably unattractive sounds.

The bells were sometimes accompanied by dancing dolls, which would twist or turn as the music played. Despite the mediocre sound of many of these boxes, they tend to be popular with collectors for their novelty value.

DUPLEX This music box, which played two cylinders on two combs simultaneously, was invented by Alfred Junod *c.*1887. There are two main types. Most commonly seen is the kind in which the cylinders and combs are arranged parallel to each other, one behind the other. The alternative arrangement is when the two cylinders are mounted in line, with the governor assembly between the two.

These very rare movements permitted a melody and an accompaniment to be played at the same time, and, by removing one cylinder, the simple melody could be played on the other.

FORTE-PIANO The forte-piano (or pianoforte) music box is believed to have been introduced by Nicole Frères in 1840. The comb was made in two separate sections, the larger piece covering approximately three-quarters of the length of the cylinder, while the smaller section made up the rest of the normal length of the comb. The sound produced had both a loud "forte" sound and a softer "piano" sound, while the combination of the two gave a double forte. Such music boxes are very rare and extremely desirable. Forte-piano music boxes made by Nicole Frères may be identified because the larger, "forte" comb has, as usual, the bass at the left and the treble notes on the right, but the "piano" comb has the treble on the left and the bass at the right.

Some of the very early boxes even combined the double comb with the mandolin effect.

Single-comb forte-piano music boxes are even rarer. One model has a comb that was tuned in such a way that many of the notes doubled or trebled, and the cylinder was pinned in such a way that all the identical notes were struck together to produce the forte effect, but only a single tooth was struck to play the piano effect. Single-comb forte-piano mechanisms are known to have been produced by Malignon and by Lecoultre & Granger.

HARPE ÉOLIENNE This term appears to have been derived from the aeolian harp – a box with an opening in it across which gut strings of varying lengths are stretched and tuned in unison, so that when air blows across them, the strings produce a sequence of rising and falling harmonies. The music boxes to which the name harpe éolienne were given did not sound much like aeolian harps, and the phrase was probably used, like the zither, as a sales tool.

These music boxes had two combs, similar in appearance to those found in the forte-piano mechanism, but the shorter comb was stiffer, although not louder, than the longer comb, and the notes it produced were used to accompany the melody. The system is thought to have been invented by the Geneva makers Conchon & Cie.

MANDOLIN In their desire to offer new refinements to the basic cylinder box, some manufacturers introduced the mandolin effect, and the lilting sound produced proved extremely popular. It was achieved by having up to eight teeth on the comb tuned to each note (or to the tones used in the tunes played) so that, by plucking each tooth in quick succession, the sound of the mandolin might be represented. Some music boxes are labeled as mandolin (or *mandoline*) when they are not true mandolin boxes. A genuine mandolin music box may be recognized by the very fine teeth of the comb and the angled lines of pins grouped in the surface of the cylinder. The pins are most obvious in the upper register, where the mandolin effect was most pronounced.

ORCHESTRA BOX This large box usually contained an organ, a comb, and a range of novelties, such as drum, bells, and castanets. Such boxes, which often have interchangeable cylinder movements, became popular after the success of the music boxes with visible bells. Reed organs, zithers, and even triangles were also sometimes included. The large, heavy boxes were made in both upright and the normal horizontal forms. In the upright models the musical movement was mounted so that the bedplate was supported vertically in a drop-fronted or double-door case while the cylinder was held horizontally.

REVOLVER BOX This curious mechanism was invented by Amédée Paillard of Sainte-Croix in 1870 and Henri Joseph Lecoultre of Geneva. The multi-cylinder box carried three, four, five, or even six cylinders on the movement itself. The name is apt, because the underlying principle is not dissimilar to that used in the six-shot revolver. The cylinders were mounted on two large wheels, one each end of the center spindle. When a wheel was rotated it brought the desired cylinder into position against the comb and locked it in place while the melody was

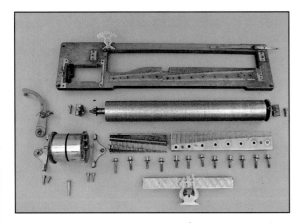

ABOVE **A sublime harmonie piccolo movement made in Switzerland, c.1880. It has been taken to pieces to show** all the component parts. The left-hand comb is turned upside-down to show the comb construction.

ABOVE **The inside surface of the spring barrel assembly, with a Geneva stop configuration, which prevents** the mechanism from being over-wound. To the right of the spring barrel a portion of the small comb is visible.

played. These mechanisms were extremely expensive to produce, and they are very rare, probably because the invention of the mechanism occurred after the introduction of the ordinary changeable cylinder, thus limiting the market for this type. They are also very heavy and large. Most known versions are by Paillard, although Nicole Frères is known also to have produced some examples.

SUBLIME HARMONIE The sublime harmonie (or harmony) box was invented by Charles Paillard. The movement depends on having two or three combs of equal length, each tuned separately but playing in harmony with each other. Paillard's patent, which was taken out in 1874 in Britain and in 1875 in the United States, was for: "a music box having several combs each of short teeth to give notes of shorter duration and also to allow slight dissonance." The music was, therefore, repeated along the length of the cylinder by the pins simultaneously striking teeth that were similar, but not identical. Music boxes that have two or more combs are not necessarily sublime harmonie mechanisms – it sometimes happened that manufacturers made combs in more than one piece because they did not have sufficient lengths of steel or because the cylinders were particularly long. A

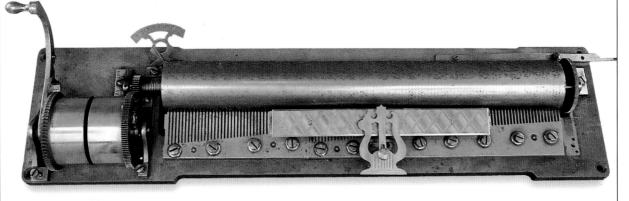

ABOVE **The same sublime movement as shown above, now assembled. The two** combs have a total of 124 teeth, 45 on the shorter comb and 79 on the other. They are placed in line so that the pins on the cylinder play the two combs at the same time. In this case one of the combs is a piccolo which enhances the sound still further.

SUBLIME HARMONIE VARIATIONS

Many variations on the basic sublime harmonie movement were subsequently introduced. All of these are pleasant to listen to and all are now extremely popular among collectors. These variations included:

▌ Sublime harmonie fortissimo, in which the combs have shorter than normal teeth. This produces a louder, somewhat strident tone.

▌ Sublime harmonie longue marche was Paillard's name for a movement that had a double co-axial spring motor that gave a very long playing time.

▌ Sublime harmonie octavo movements had the second comb tuned a full octave higher than the first.

▌ Sublime harmonie piccolo was, perhaps, the most popular arrangement for medium-sized, interchangeable cylinder boxes, and it is, therefore, the most likely to be encountered by collectors. In addition to the two combs, a third, small comb at the treble end was tuned to a higher pitch, heightening still further the sounds that were produced. The Geneva company Mojon, Manger & Co. made many of these mechanisms.

▌ Sublime harmonie tremolo had an additional third comb, tuned to give a mandolin affect. The tremolo harmonique was similar to the standard sublime harmonie, but the second comb was shorter and tuned higher than the first.

sublime harmonie mechanism may be recognized by the fact that the treble end of the first comb is adjacent to the bass end of the next comb.

ZITHER ATTACHMENT The zither attachment, which was also sometimes known as the harp attachment, was positioned over the comb. It consisted of a mounting fixture with a hinged bracket and bar. Underneath the bar was a roll of stiff tissue paper. The fixture would be mounted in such a way that the bar was suspended over the teeth of the comb. When the bar was lowered, the roll of tissue paper acted as a damper and caused the sounds produced to be modified slightly. The attachment was controlled manually, and on old music boxes this can cause problems, because if the tissue paper has been left resting against the comb for too long, the paper may become stuck to the teeth or, by absorbing moisture, cause the comb to rust.

The zither attachment was introduced in the 1880s and proved enormously popular. It was supposed to enhance the sound, although in fact the buzzing noise produced was nothing like the sound of the zither, and even less like the sound of the harp. Even so, some manufacturers, especially of cheaper boxes, included large and impressive-looking zithers.

Some makers designed and built music boxes with automatic zithers, in which the attachment was an integral part of the mechanism and was controlled by cams built into the cylinder. As the music played, the zither was raised or lowered to add some variation to the sound.

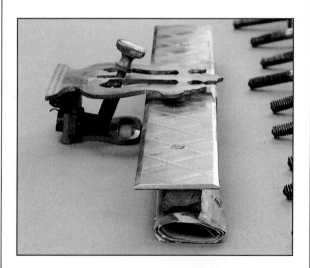

ABOVE **A side view of the zither attachment, which is placed so that it is positioned over the teeth of the comb. The lever used to raise or lower the zither extends from the decorative lyre-shaped fixture in the center of the bar.**

THE INTERCHANGEABLE DISC MUSIC BOX

C H A P T E R 2

The development in the mid-1880s of the interchangeable disc music box, with its inexpensive discs, heralded the decline of the cylinder music box. In fact, the disc music box had a short life. The first disc-playing music boxes appeared in 1885, but by 1914 the industry had virtually vanished.

In simple terms, the disc music box is a wooden case enclosing a musical movement that employs projections or holes on an interchangeable, revolving metal disc. The projections or holes cause star wheels to turn, which strike the tuned teeth of a metal comb or combs in the desired sequence. The bedplate assembly consists of the comb or combs, the star wheel assembly that plucks them, and the dampers and brakes that control the combs and wheels. The motor assembly contains the driving force – the center drive or the peripheral drive – the speed of which is controlled by a series of wheels terminating in an endless screw. The endless screw is fitted with an air brake.

The disc music box had really begun in the early years of the 19th century, with mechanisms that used a fixed rotating disc. This type of mechanism had been incorporated into small, flat objects such as snuff-boxes and pocket watches, and it was, as we have seen, the forerunner of the cylinder music box. However, the development of a removable, interchangeable disc mechanism proved to be a major breakthrough, and almost from the moment of their first appearance, these music boxes, which were less expensive and louder, and offered a greater choice of tunes than the cylinder music box, captured the public's interest. One of the first people to patent a design for a practical disc machine seems to have

LEFT **A Mira 18½in (46.5cm) disc made around 1900. The outer edge of the disc has a reinforcing lip. Mira disc music boxes were made by the Swiss manufacturer** Mermod Frères, and the actions were shipped to distributors in Europe and the United States who fitted the mechanisms into locally made cabinets.

been Ellis Parr of London, but the first interchangeable disc music box was produced in Germany, and German companies continued to dominate the market, although manufacturers in both Switzerland and, later, the United States also produced models.

Among the many names involved in the production of the disc music box, perhaps the best known are Symphonion, Polyphon, and Regina. Symphonion and Polyphon were German companies, while Regina was based in the United States. Between them they were responsible for

approximately 90 per cent of the total market, and they produced hundreds of thousands of boxes. At one time Polyphon had more than 1,000 employees, while Symphonion employed about 400 people. Regina, which alone produced about 100,000 disc music boxes, employed more than 350 people.

At first, metal discs with projections on the underside were developed. The first of these were zinc, and the projections often became brittle and snapped off as the metal aged. Around 1895 most manufacturers changed to steel discs, although a few

LEFT **The same Mira model with the lid open to show the unusual pressure arm mechanism for changing discs.**

BELOW **A cabinet-style floor-standing Mira disc player, which was made for home use and takes 18½in (46.5cm) discs. The colorful decorations are actually decals. The lid is lifted to reveal the disc player, while the base of the unit contains the disc storage area.**

LEFT **Two 15½in (39.5cm) Regina discs. The right-hand disc is made of zinc. The Regina Music Box Co. was founded in Rahway, New Jersey, in 1892, and between that date and 1921 the company produced 100,000 music boxes, claiming between 80 and 90 percent of the US market.**

continued to use zinc alloy, which did not become brittle with age. Discs without projections began to be made *c*.1895. These turned the star wheel by allowing the point of the star to protrude through a slot. As the disc revolved, it would turn the star wheel and cause it to pluck the note. Perhaps the best known of the machines to use discs without projections was the Stella. The mechanism required to achieve this was quite different from the ones that used discs with projections.

One of the major problems confronting disc box manufacturers was to find an effective and long-lasting means of damping the notes before they could be struck again. Many different styles were tried. Polyphon, for example, used at least six different kinds in its 15½in (39.5cm) mechanisms. Eventually, most manufacturers adopted a method that incorporated D-shaped dampers that ran vertically between the teeth from a brass bar. This system proved so successful that disc music boxes can be found today in which the dampers still function perfectly.

The basic configuration in the interchangeable disc music box was the single comb. Automatic disc-changing mechanisms were soon developed, and although Regina was the leader in this field, it was Polyphon who had actually been the first to perfect the system.

In 1896 a mechanism was patented that permitted two tunes to be played from the same disc. At the end of the first revolution of the disc, the center spindle would shift slightly and align a different set of projections so that a second tune could be played. Mermod Frères of Sainte-Croix produced units using this patent in the New Century series.

Upright disc music boxes, in which the disc is mounted vertically, were made in both table and floor-standing models. The upright style was popular for commercial use, and many coin-operated examples are found.

In an effort to compete with the phonograph, several models were produced that were able to play discs and, by the use of an attachment, could also be used as a phonograph. However, the campaigns mounted in the early 1900s by companies such as the Victor Talking Machine Co. to sell phonographs were successful, and disc boxes ceased to be made.

Many different styles of disc music box were produced, and the names of the main kinds are listed in Chapter 7. However, because they dominated the market and because their music boxes are so widely collected today, the three main manufacturers, Symphonion, Polyphon, and Regina, are discussed here. There is also a brief description of some of the more unusual mechanisms and styles of disc music box.

SYMPHONION

The Leipzig company, Kuhno-Lochmann, which was founded by Paul Lochmann, was the first commercial manufacturer of a disc machine. Lochmann had manufactured various kinds of machinery before turning to disc music boxes with the opening of the Symphonion factory. The first Symphonion was produced in 1886, and it was an immediate success. Leipzig became the center of the disc music box industry in Europe, and remained so until the industry declined.

The Symphonion was produced in a wide variety of sizes, types, and styles, and the company, which had been reorganized and renamed as Symphonion Fabrik Lochmannscher Musikwerke, was responsible for many of the developments and innovations that occurred. In 1888 the company was employing 120 people in its factory, and many of the discs were made by out-workers, mostly women, in their own homes. In 1903 the company reported that it was producing between 5,000 and 6,000 machines and 100,000 discs a year. As many as 21 different sizes have been identified, ranging from 4½in (11cm) to 30in (76cm), although the differences between some of these are so slight as to make it difficult to distinguish among them. Some sizes were produced for only a short period – the 10⅝in (27.5cm) disc, for example, seems to have been produced only in the early years of the company's existence. Several of the sizes used peripheral dimple-drive discs – the 13¼in (34cm) and 27⅝in (70cm), for example – and the smallest size, the 4½in (11cm), was used in small clocks. Pinion-driven discs may be identified by their serrated edges.

During the 1890s, which were the heyday of the disc music box, Symphonion introduced several different styles of disc-playing clocks, and it also produced very successful multiple disc machines, of which the three-disc Eroica had a distinctive and attractive sound. The Rococo, which used a normal 11⅞in (30cm) disc, was contained in an attractively carved wooden case. The Gambrinus, which also

BELOW A 27½in (70cm) Symphonion disc, c.1896. The Symphonion, made by Paul Lochmann of Leipzig, was the first practical disc music box to be made. The dimples, which were used instead of holes to engage with the drive wheel to turn the disc, are visible at the outer edge of the disc.

ABOVE A close-up view of the 12 bells on an Imperial Symphonion, which was made by the Symphonion Manufacturing Co. of New Jersey. This was a branch of the Leipzig company, Symphonion Fabrik Lochmannscher Musikwerke. The US plant was established in 1896–7 to supply the growing market for music boxes. This unit features 12 bells.

housed a mechanism playing a 11⅞in (30cm) disc, was a coin-operated machine, designed to stand on a bar in a beer cellar, and was made in the shape of a beer barrel. Advertisements suggest that by 1902 Symphonion was making an automatic disc-change music box that played 25in (63cm) discs, but none so far has been found.

In 1896–7 Symphonion established a subsidiary in the United States – the Imperial Symphonion Manufacturing Co. at Bradley Beach, New Jersey. At first music boxes were imported from Germany, but wholly US-made versions of the disc music box known as the Imperial Symphonion were being made by 1898. The Imperial Symphonions, which were somewhat similar in appearance to the Regina, included a three-disc machine, which was completely unlike anything that was available in Germany.

Many collectors consider that the tone of Symphonion music boxes, especially the 19⅛in (48.5cm), was superior to the Polyphon models,.

Symphonion also opened showrooms in London in 1900, but the products offered by this time included phonographs and other pieces of musical equipment.

During 1900 Lochmann himself opened a new factory, the Original Musikwerke Paul Lochmann GmbH, at Zeulenroda in central Germany, where he made the Lochmann Original series of disc music boxes and the disc-playing orchestrion known as the Original Konzert Piano.

POLYPHON

The Polyphon Musikwerke was established by Gustave Brachhausen *c.*1889. Brachhausen had worked for Symphonion, but he and a colleague, Paul Reissner, decided to set up in opposition to Lochmann, establishing a factory not far from their former employer.

Possibly because Polyphon was better at marketing and selling than Symphonion, it quickly

ABOVE **This original 22⅛in (56cm) Polyphon disc was manufactured for use in the company's table-top Casket Model.**

outstripped the older company in both production and sales. In addition, most of the pioneering work had been carried out by Symphonion – zinc alloy discs could be made stronger by using two pieces of metal cut from the disc, with one bent down behind the other to provide additional support, and, most importantly, Symphonion's Paul Wendland had invented the star wheel in 1889. Polyphon, therefore, was well placed to take advantage of the growing market.

One innovation the company did make, however, was to make yet stronger discs by cutting a single tongue from the metal and bending it over to the surface of the disc, almost in the form of a bridge. Although Lochmann contested Polyphon's use of this as an infringement of his patent in a lengthy court case, Polyphon eventually won.

The company produced many clocks fitted with disc movements, and these were often coin-operated. So successful was the company that in 1899 it moved to larger premises to accommodate the increasing numbers of people it was employing.

The company's range of models included 19⅝in (50.5cm), 22in (56cm) and 24½in (62cm) disc mechanisms housed in upright cabinets, some with, some without disc bins. There was even a very rare "folding-top" table box. Examples of Polyphon music boxes have been found housed in original bookcases, china cabinets, and bureaux, and although the company appears to have limited the number of discs it used to 14, these were housed in a bewildering variety of cabinets. There was also an automatic change model.

The company introduced the Polyphon-Concerto *c.*1900. This was a disc orchestrion that played a piano, bass drum, snare drum, and glockenspiel. Many of these were imported into the United States by Regina (see page 24). Later models of the Concerto played paper rolls, and disc or roll models were offered as a choice.

A basic table or upright Polyphon was made with an attachment to play the new phonograph discs. This model, the Gramo-Polyphon, could play either music box discs or the new phonograph discs, and it was also made, extremely successfully, by Regina. However, the model was a harbinger of what was to come, and by 1914 Polyphon had ceased production of disc music boxes.

RIGHT **This rare table version of the Polyphon is often called the Casket Model because of the double-hinged lid and the shape of the closed case. It is 28½ × 17 × 11in (72 × 43 × 28cm).**

RIGHT **The Casket Model 22⅛in (56cm) disc Polyphon is shown here with its double-hinged top open. The duplex combs and the 16 bells that accompany the tune are clearly visible. The basic tuned combs have a total of 60 teeth. At the end of these are the small combs that play the bells; each of these small combs has eight teeth. This model is especially interesting in that there is a spiral spring instead of the more conventional coil-wound spring.**

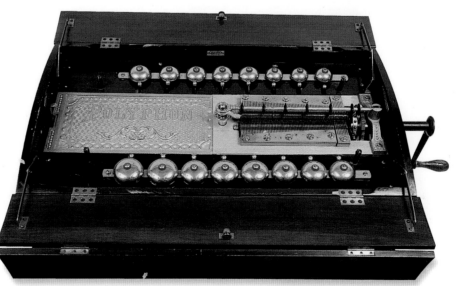

REGINA

Many collectors consider that the Regina disc music box has the best sound of all. In addition, the cabinets in which the mechanisms are housed are widely admired for their craftsmanship and style.

The company was established in 1892, when Polyphon's founder, Gustave Brachhausen, went to the United States to found the Regina Music Box Co., in Jersey City. For several years Polyphon supplied parts and discs that were assembled in America and marketed by Regina. Eventually however, an increasing number of discs and mechanisms were made at the Jersey City factory. However, because of the early cooperation between the two companies, many discs up to and including 15½in (39.5cm) are interchangeable between Regina and Polyphon music boxes. It seems likely

ABOVE **A 15½in (39.5cm) Regina disc. This is a typical metal disc showing the slots** **that remain after the projections were made for the tune arrangement.**

that the larger, mostly coin-operated machines were not made until the late 1890s, which would explain why the larger discs are not interchangeable, for by this time Regina was making its own mechanisms.

When the automatic disc changing mechanism was developed in 1897 Regina began to service and collect the money from the coin-operated machines it supplied, also changing the discs. These machines played 15½in (39.5cm), 20¾in (53cm) and 27in (68.5cm) discs.

At the height of its success Regina was making $2 million a year, but by 1903 the competition from disc phonographs was beginning to have its effect. Regina tried to diversify, including making a hand-operated vacuum-cleaner in 1902. In 1903 it began to import the disc orchestrions from Polyphon, and these used discs of 32in (82cm) and played piano, tuned tubular bells, drum, and triangle. The Reginaphone had a turntable and a horn that could be removed, and the phonograph arm could be turned to one side so that it could be used as a normal music box. Regina also made some models with the horn built into the case. However, although the company continued to make music boxes until 1919, it never regained its share of the market, and in 1922 it went bankrupt.

BELOW **A Regina 15½in (39.5cm) disc player in a mahogany case, c.1900. Note** **the picture on the inside surface of the lid.**

Unlike many manufacturers of disc music boxes, Regina kept detailed records of styles, serial numbers, dates of manufacture, and so on, and it is, therefore, possible for collectors to be able accurately to identify the provenance of the company's machines.

MODIFICATIONS TO THE DISC MUSIC BOX

Just as the popularity of cylinder music boxes encouraged the manufacturers to introduce novelties and to try to refine and improve the basic system, so the popularity of disc boxes led to several additions.

AUTOMATIC DISC-CHANGERS In these machines the disc title can be selected, a coin inserted in a slot or a lever pulled, and the disc is lifted from its storage rack, placed on the playing mechanism, and then, when the tune has finished, returned to the rack. The system is thought to have been invented by Gustave Brachhausen in 1897, when he was running Regina in the United States.

Polyphon disc-change machines were made in 15½in (39.5cm), 19⅝in (50.5cm), which seems to have been the most popular, 22in (56cm) and 24½in (62cm) models, and many of these are coin-operated. Regina produced 15½in (39.5cm), 20¾in (53cm) and 27in (68.5cm) versions. Symphonion is believed to have made a model, but none has been found.

BELLS Unlike the bells that were included in the cylinder boxes, the bells added to disc movements tended to be used on existing combs. Tuned metal bars or tubular bells (rather than the conventionally shaped bell of the cylinder box), were played by an arrangement added to the outer edge of the disc; the discs were larger, but the comb remained the same size. Some models had extra levers or sections of untuned comb added to the end of the star wheel assembly, and depressing the levers made it possible to remove the bell accompaniment.

On the smallest, often hand-turned boxes, the bells were hidden beneath the bedplate. The Symphonion 27in (68.5cm) and the Polyphon 22in (56cm) discs used tubular bells, and these were normally housed in upright models. However, the Emerald, a very rare 22in (56cm) disc music box made by Polyphon, is a table-mounted machine. The Regina 216 music box played a 15½in (39.5cm) disc on a 124-tooth double-comb mechanism, and a special disc was required to play the 12 bells, six mounted on either side of the disc mechanism. These discs may be identified by the legend *For Bell Instrument Only* and the two bells near the bottom. The unit itself measured 22 × 18¾ × 13in (56 × 47.5 × 33cm).

Other boxes were built with combinations of bells, triangles, drums, reeds, and even piano strings.

CLOCKS Discs were often incorporated into clocks so that a tune was played on the hour. Both the 4½in (11cm) Symphonion disc and the 24½in (62cm) Polyphon disc were used in this way. Regina often included a 15½in (39.5cm) disc in a clock case that was over 8ft (2.4m) tall. All such clocks are desirable.

DUPLEX COMBS Double or, more properly, duplex combs were two matching combs, which were mounted opposite each other, one on either side of the star wheel. Some of these combs had pairs of teeth that were tuned an octave apart. As the star wheel turns, it plucks the same notes on each comb. Although this system did not, as might have been thought, double the volume – the increase was only about 25 per cent – it did produce a more pleasing, mellower tone.

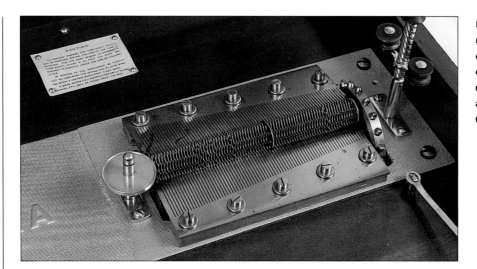

LEFT **A Regina movement made in 1898 with duplex combs for a 15½in (39.5cm) disc. The pressure arm is raised so that the star wheel arrangement in the center of the two combs is visible.**

FORTUNA "ORGAN BOX" The Fortuna, which was a forerunner of the orchestrion, was manufactured by J. H. Zimmerman of Leipzig. This was an upright machine that played a 26in (66cm) disc, and included a musical steel comb, a set of harmonium reeds, a triangle, and a drum. It was available both with and without a disc store, and the double doors were either carved or fretted. These are very rare machines, and are highly sought after among collectors.

MULTIPLE-DISC MACHINES These machines generally played two discs, which were arranged to play in harmony with each other. Symphonion produced two- and three-disc machines, and Paul Lochmann also made a large, upright two-disc model after he had left Symphonion. The Lochmann Original is 5ft (1.5m) long and plays 24½in (62cm) discs; it also has bells. The Gloria, which was made by the Swiss consortium Société Anonyme, played two discs in an upright case.

Polyphon's entry into this area was marked by the production of a 24½in (62cm) double-disc player, and Zimmermann, the manufacturer of the Fortuna, also appears to have manufactured a double-disc model. Symphonion produced table-standing double-disc players, and the most commonly found of the multiple-disc music boxes is Symphonion's Eroica, which played three discs.

MULTIPLE-TUNE DISCS In an attempt to overcome the tedium of having to play the same disc over and over again, and before the automatic disc-change system was introduced, two manufacturers, Gustav Bortmann and Alfred Kelier, patented a disc that played two tunes, each tune playing a full turn of the disc. This was marketed as the Sirion, and the change in tune was achieved by shifting the center spindle so that a second set of projections was brought into play. The Sirion was available in upright and table versions and is very rare.

SUBLIME HARMONIE COMB This effect was achieved by the use of two combs and star wheels, mounted on each side of the center spindle. The configuration caused the disc to have twice the number of projections or slots as a single or regular duplex comb mode. The intention was the same as the introduction of the sublime harmonie in the cylinder box (see Chapter 1).

ZITHER The zither attachment was popular between *c.*1900 and 1910. It served the same purpose as the zither attachment on the cylinder music box.

UNDERSTANDING YOUR MUSIC BOX

CHAPTER 3

As your interest in music boxes, whether cylinder or disc, develops, you will become increasingly familiar with the terminology used to describe the different parts of the mechanism. Some of the basic features of cylinder and disc music boxes are described in this chapter, but the following terms are those that apply to both kinds of mechanism.

BEDPLATE – the base on which the components – cylinder, comb, governor, and so on – are held. The bedplate is the means by which the unit is fixed inside its case or housing.

BRIDGES – brackets at either end of the cylinder and spring barrel that are used to mount the mechanism.

CASE – the box or cabinet in which the mechanism is housed. A well-constructed case and mounting will amplify the sound.

COMB – a series of teeth or prongs that produce the desired notes. When the steel that is used to make the comb is cut and shaped to produce the teeth, it resembles an ordinary comb. The prongs or teeth may be thought of as miniature tuning forks that generate a particular note when they are struck.

DAMPER – the means by which the vibration of a tooth is stopped just before the tooth is played again. If a second note is played while a tooth is still vibrating because the pin or star wheel comes into contact with the vibrating tooth, an additional noise will be produced, and this is usually described as a buzzing, scraping, or screeching sound.

DUPLEX – the word used to describe a music box that plays two combs or two cylinders simultaneously.

ENDLESS SCREW – this is located in the governor mechanism and is the heart of the governor. It looks like an ordinary screw with a shaft protruding from

LEFT **A typical disc player made by Regina around 1895, with the 15½in (39.5cm)** mechanism housed in an elegant carved wood case finished in mahogany.

each end. The wings of the governor are attached to the upper shaft of the screw, and these wings act as an air brake, helping to control the speed of the movement.

GEAR TRAIN – the sequence of wheels and pinions that transmit power between the spring or power source and the endless screw.

GOVERNOR – the device that controls the power and speed of the turning cylinder or disc. The governor may be distinguished by the wings that turn when the music box plays.

KEY, CRANK, OR WINDING LEVER – the handle attached to the motor that is used to wind the spring. Cranks are used to turn the mechanism manually.

MAINSPRING – the steel spring that provides the power to turn the movement.

MOVEMENT OR MECHANISM – the completed assembly of parts and components (governor, motor, bedplate, cylinder, and so on) required to produce a tune.

PROJECTIONS – the points that are stamped out of a disc or cylinder. The projections turn either the star wheel of a disc mechanism or pluck the tooth of a cylinder movement. Cylinder boxes with projections (in place of the traditional pins) have been used only since 1925.

SPRINGMOTOR OR MOTOR – the housing (spring barrel), spring unit, and gearing that powers the mechanism.

CYLINDER MUSIC BOXES

When people think of a music box they tend to think of the cylinder-type mechanism, in which the tune is played by a revolving cylinder. The pins on the cylinder pluck the teeth on a fixed comb to create the tones. The power to play these mechanisms comes from a spring, whose power is directed through gears, and it is the gears that turn the cylinder and the governor.

Like watches, music boxes could not be made until the spring had been invented. The first mechanical time-keeper which was truly portable is thought to have been made by Peter Henlein of Nürnberg *c.*1510. Even though the motive power provided by the spring was constant, early watches were inaccurate until the balance-spring was invented *c.*1675 by Christian Huyghens or Robert Hooke, and the same problem applied to music boxes, whose cylinders ran more slowly as the spring ran down.

BELOW **A Kalliope 20½in (52cm) coin-operated, table-mounted disc player with 12 bells made *c.*1896.** Immediately beneath the unit is a drawer that allowed access to the coin box.

GOVERNOR ASSEMBLY

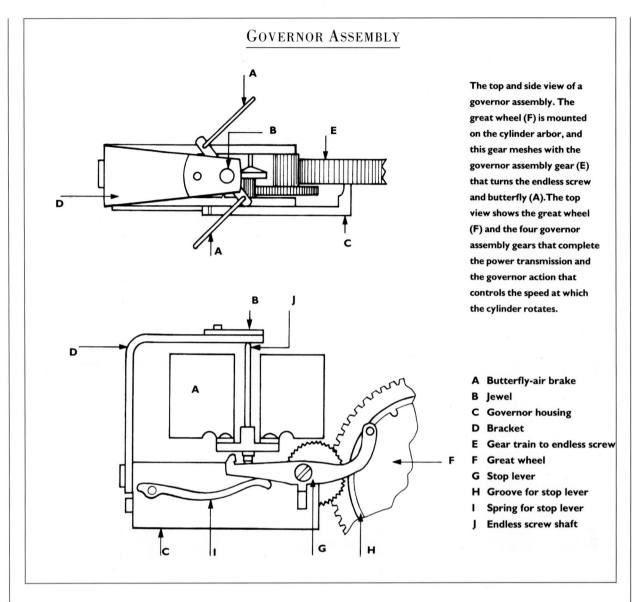

The top and side view of a governor assembly. The great wheel (F) is mounted on the cylinder arbor, and this gear meshes with the governor assembly gear (E) that turns the endless screw and butterfly (A). The top view shows the great wheel (F) and the four governor assembly gears that complete the power transmission and the governor action that controls the speed at which the cylinder rotates.

A Butterfly-air brake
B Jewel
C Governor housing
D Bracket
E Gear train to endless screw
F Great wheel
G Stop lever
H Groove for stop lever
I Spring for stop lever
J Endless screw shaft

BUTTERFLY ASSEMBLY

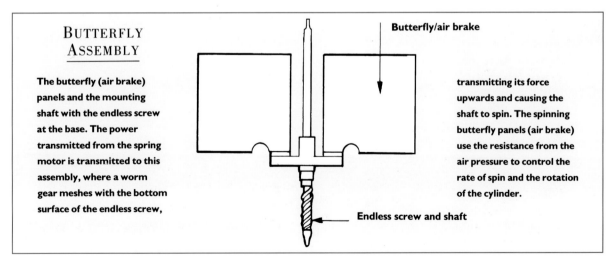

The butterfly (air brake) panels and the mounting shaft with the endless screw at the base. The power transmitted from the spring motor is transmitted to this assembly, where a worm gear meshes with the bottom surface of the endless screw, transmitting its force upwards and causing the shaft to spin. The spinning butterfly panels (air brake) use the resistance from the air pressure to control the rate of spin and the rotation of the cylinder.

Butterfly/air brake

Endless screw and shaft

COMB – BACK VIEW

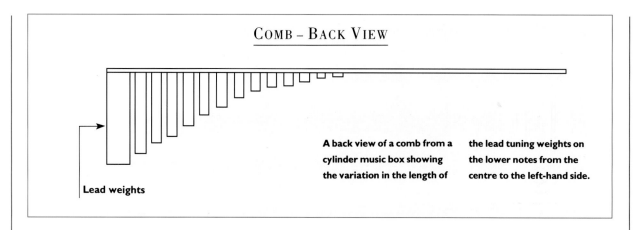

Lead weights

A back view of a comb from a cylinder music box showing the variation in the length of the lead tuning weights on the lower notes from the centre to the left-hand side.

COMBS The number of teeth on a comb can vary considerably. Most music boxes made today have between six and eighteen notes, and a wide range of tunes can be produced from that number of teeth. The top quality cylinder music boxes, which have a superior musical mechanism and produce a better sound, may have anywhere between 28 and 144 teeth.

If you look at a comb you will notice that the individual teeth differ in length and width. Just as in a grand piano, where the longest and thickest strings produce the bass notes and the finer, shorter strings produce the higher notes, so in a music box the higher notes are produced by the narrower and shorter teeth, and the bass notes are produced by the longer, thicker teeth.

However, because the size of the music box case is limited, the lower notes are produced by adding weights to the underside of the teeth. If you remove the mechanism from the case and look at it from underneath you will see that, from about the middle of the range, the teeth have a little platform towards the end. This additional weight lowers the note produced by the tooth. Lead tuning weights can be attached to the platform to lower the note still further, and tuning weights are often found in music boxes with more than 18 teeth.

TEETH

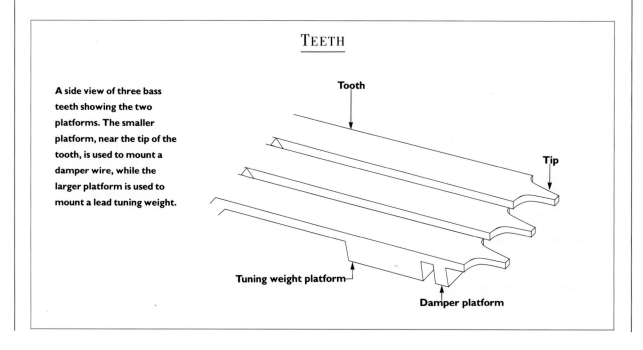

A side view of three bass teeth showing the two platforms. The smaller platform, near the tip of the tooth, is used to mount a damper wire, while the larger platform is used to mount a lead tuning weight.

Tooth

Tip

Tuning weight platform

Damper platform

COMB – FRONT VIEW

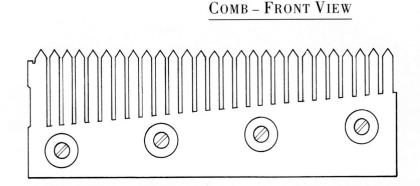

A comb showing the varying lengths of the teeth, with the extra-wide bass tooth.

Final tuning is achieved by adding weight to or taking it from the end of the tooth. Some teeth are filed to achieve the correct note.

Because each comb is made and tuned to produce a particular set of notes, the tune in a cylinder music box cannot be changed unless the box was specifically made to take interchangeable cylinders.

Dampers for cylinder boxes are attached to the lower surface of the tooth of the comb in such a way that when a pin is about to pluck the tooth, the damper is raised and touches the tooth, so stopping any vibration from the previous note. The damper is aligned so that it is released just before the pin actually plucks the tooth, so allowing a clear note to be sounded. Before the new nylon dampers were available, chicken feathers were used as dampers on the finest teeth.

CYLINDERS The apparently natural wish to have music boxes that played more than one tune led, first, to the development of the two-tune cylinder – that is, two tunes were played one after the other on

TOOTH CROSS-SECTION

A cross-section of a tooth showing the section from the damper platform to the front end of the tooth. An extremely small hole, less than $\frac{1}{32}$in (1mm) in diameter, is drilled into the damper platform at point A. A damper wire is placed in the hole and extended forwards to the front of the tooth in a bow shape. A brass taper pin is inserted at point A to hold the damper wire in place, while the damper wire is manually shaped and positioned so that the tip of the wire is slightly behind and below the tip of the tooth.

When a cylinder pin comes into contact with the wire, it pushes it upwards so that it touches the tooth and stops it from vibrating; this is done because if a cylinder pin comes into contact with an already vibrating tooth it can cause a high-pitched squeal. Because the wire is positioned just below the tooth, as the pin moves upwards, the wire is released before the cylinder pin touches and raises the tooth, so ensuring that the tooth creates a clean, clear tone when it is released by the pin.

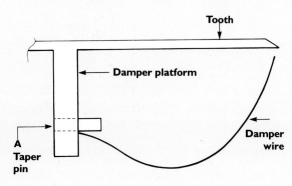

Tooth

Damper platform

A
Taper
pin

Damper
wire

ABOVE **The movement and compartment dividers of this 1880 music box are shown in front of the case. The assembled movement, minus the governor, has a long cylinder, a double-barreled spring motor assembly, comb, and tune counter attached to the gold-painted bedplate. Wooden screws were used to fasten the bedplate to the case. In front and at each end of the movement can be seen the panel units used to separate the case into three sections. The left-hand compartment contained the winding lever; the right-hand compartment housed the control lever and cover.**

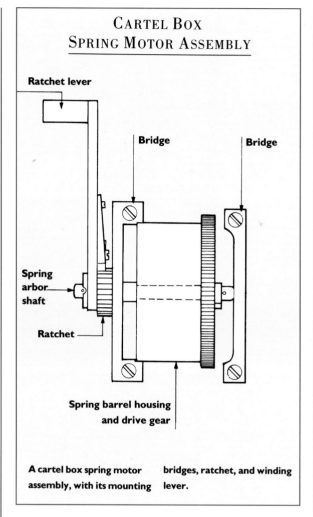

CARTEL BOX SPRING MOTOR ASSEMBLY

Ratchet lever

Bridge

Bridge

Spring arbor shaft

Ratchet

Spring barrel housing and drive gear

A cartel box spring motor assembly, with its mounting bridges, ratchet, and winding lever.

the same cylinder. However, as long as the diameter of the cylinder remained unchanged, both tunes were, necessarily, fairly short.

The next step was to increase the diameter of the cylinder, so that longer or more tunes could be played. Perhaps the most keenly collected of this type of music box are the overture or *ouverture* boxes, which played from two to eight operatic overtures on a single cylinder. Such boxes are rare. Not only do they have larger diameter cylinders – they may range from 3½ to 4in (9–10cm) – but they also have very fine combs. Nicole Frères and Lecoultre Frères are known to have made them. Some of the larger boxes had as many as 300 teeth on a comb, and some of the top quality examples had

brass or silver tune sheets. The Grand (or *Grande*) Format Overture Box, which had a very large musical movement and a cylinder 18–22in (45.5–56cm) long and 4½–5in (11–12.5cm) wide, was made by Nicole Frères and Heller, and Lecoultre is known to have made even larger examples. Some large diameter cylinders had as many as 3,000 pins.

One large diameter cylinder box that was not an overture mechanism was known as the American box. It was made during the 1890s, and its name derives from the American eagle on the lid. As many as 20 or 30 tunes could be played by the "two tunes a turn" method, but unfortunately these mechanisms do not produce a good tone and the tunes were badly arranged.

BASIC CARTEL MOVEMENT

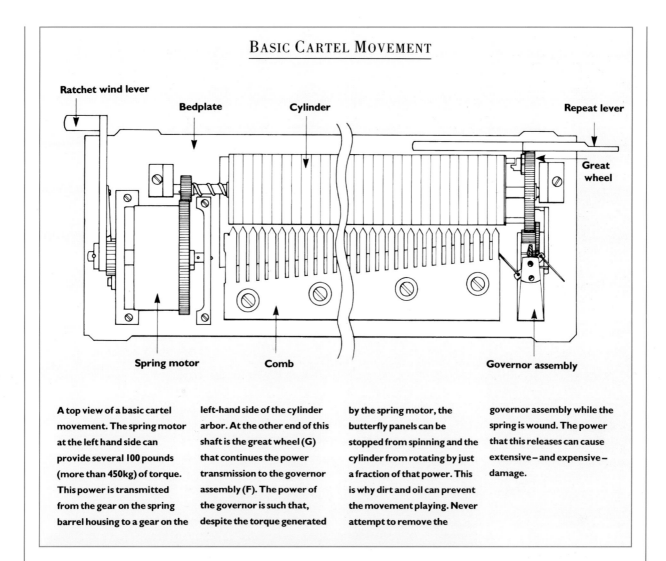

Ratchet wind lever

Bedplate

Cylinder

Repeat lever

Great wheel

Spring motor

Comb

Governor assembly

A top view of a basic cartel movement. The spring motor at the left hand side can provide several 100 pounds (more than 450kg) of torque. This power is transmitted from the gear on the spring barrel housing to a gear on the left-hand side of the cylinder arbor. At the other end of this shaft is the great wheel (G) that continues the power transmission to the governor assembly (F). The power of the governor is such that, despite the torque generated by the spring motor, the butterfly panels can be stopped from spinning and the cylinder from rotating by just a fraction of that power. This is why dirt and oil can prevent the movement playing. Never attempt to remove the governor assembly while the spring is wound. The power that this releases can cause extensive – and expensive – damage.

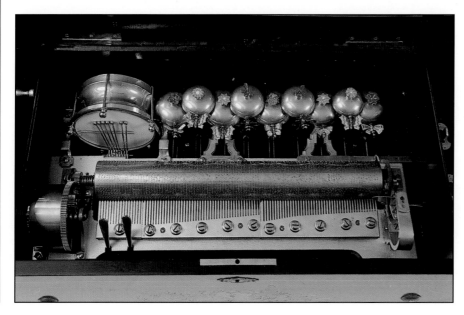

LEFT The open lid of this orchestra box reveals the large cylinder movement together with the additional novelty features of the decorative bells and the bee strikers, and, mounted to the left of the bells, the drum and its series of beaters. In the left-hand corner of the case the tops of two levers are visible: these are extra controls to activate the playing of the bells and drum.

LEFT **These two multi-tune music boxes, which date from the 1940s, were made by Cuendet. Each movement plays more than one tune by moving the cylinder. The box on the left has a movement with 30 teeth and a cylinder 1¾in (4.5cm) long; it plays two tunes – "The Bat" and "Rosen from the South". The box on the right has 44 teeth and a cylinder that is 2½in (6cm) long; it plays three different tunes – "Un Tour de Valse", "Beim Souper", and "Über den Wellen". Both movements are different lengths, but the case sizes are the same: 5½ × 3½ × 2¾in (14 × 9 × 7cm). Note the tune sheets on the inside of the lids.**

BELOW **An interchangeable cartel box by Reuge, c.1980, which is described as follows in their catalogue: "Perfected around 1885 in Sainte-Croix, this interchangeable cylinder system has the invaluable advantage of considerably increasing the number of tunes and length of the music. The double comb composed of 144 teeth plays over a range of five octaves. The unit comes with five interchangeable cylinders, each having four tunes."**

Another way in which the number of tunes could be increased was to lengthen the cylinder so that several airs could be placed side by side. At the end of the first tune, the cylinder would shift sideways to play the next tune.

The interchangeable cylinder, which allowed several cylinders to be used on the same basic movement, was, however, the most important development in increasing the number of tunes that could be played. These interchangeable cylinders – *pièces à rechange* – first appeared *c.*1850, and it was possible to buy the extra cylinders only with the machine for which they were intended. The earliest examples appear to have been made by the Swiss maker Ducommun-Girod, and six cylinders were supplied with the mechanism, which was housed in a rather plain-looking case.

Interchangeable cylinders, which could be obtained separately and which could be used on a series of boxes, all made to the same specifications, did not appear until later. These boxes were often supplied with a matching table with a drawer in which the extra cylinders could be stored, making the music box into a piece of furniture in its own right. The movements of interchangeable cylinder boxes are distinctive because there is always a mounting and clamping device that allows the removal and replacement of the cylinder.

A variation of the interchangeable cylinder was the interchangeable cylinder sleeve. Instead of having to purchase an entire cylinder, it was possible to buy a much less expensive sleeve. The system, known as the Alexandra, was patented by Alfred Junod, Jules Jaccard and Paul Calame Jaccard in 1891.

SAFETY DEVICES The basic purpose of the safety check is to prevent the cylinder from turning so quickly that the governor mechanism is disengaged. If the governor is disengaged while the spring is

under tension, the power of the spring will be released unchecked. This uncontrolled power will cause the cylinder to spin very fast, and this may damage the pins on the cylinder and the teeth of the comb. This action, which is known as a "run," may cause damage that is extremely costly to repair or, even, that is beyond repair.

Several mechanisms were developed that came into action as soon as the cylinder began to turn too quickly. Charles Henry Jacot, one of three brothers living in the United States, was active in devising safety checks. Jacot's "Patent Safety Check," which first appeared in 1885, worked on gravity. A large ratchet wheel was fixed to the end of the cylinder, and a special double-toothed pawl (a lever with a catch for the teeth of a wheel) with a weighted arm rested against the wheel. As the box played, the arm

THE PARTS OF A CYLINDER MUSIC BOX

CYLINDER – the tube assembly that holds the pins and their musical arrangement. It consists of removable end plates, an arbor (or shaft), interior reinforcing rings if necessary, and a composition material (known as cement) that holds and anchors the pins in position.

GENEVA STOP – the device mounted on the spring barrel to prevent the spring from being over-wound. It also stops the spring from winding down too far. The device consists of two specially shaped round metal discs, one of which is mounted over the end of the spring arbor shaft while the second is mounted on the spring barrel. When the disc mounted on the arbor shaft comes into contact with the stop position of the second disc, the arbor is prevented from turning any further.

GREAT WHEEL – the large gear that transmits power from the cylinder assembly to the governor.

PINS – wires that are inserted into holes drilled in the cylinder. They strike the tooth or prong of the comb to generate the tone for the required note.

TUNE SHEET – the list of tunes that are played on a music box, usually found mounted on the inside of the lid. These are sometimes the only way in which the manufacturer may be identified.

ABOVE **The open lid of this box, which was made around 1880, reveals the original and colorful tune sheet. The on/ off and repeat controls can be seen on the right and the ratchet wind crank lever on** the left. The center compartment contains the mechanism and features a hinged glass lid. The brightly finished tune counter with its red center is visible at the back left-hand side of the mechanism.

alternately engaged and disengaged pawls. If the speed at which the cylinder was turning increased, the weighted pawl would jam the ratchet wheel and hold the cylinder firm. Another method, the Parachute, was devised by Mermod Frères of Sainte-Croix. This worked on the same principle, but the rocking pawl became a feature of the movement, and was fitted with a shield bearing Mermod Frères' trademark.

Paillard used a system that depended on centrifugal force. A small pinion was positioned so that it was rotated by the cylinder's great wheel. The pinion turned a shaft through which was bored a cross hole, and through this hole was balanced a rod with a steel ball at one end and a compression spring at the other. When the cylinder turned slowly, the rod remained balanced, but if the cylinder turned too quickly, the ball would be moved outwards so that the rod jammed against the attachment bracket of the great wheel.

TUNE INDICATOR A tune indicator would be fitted on both interchangeable and fixed cylinder boxes. It consisted of a pointer that moved against a piece of metal to show the number of the tune being played. When the cylinder shifted to play a new tune, the lower end of the pointer would be pulled by a small spring against the end of the cylinder. Tune indicators were usually positioned at the end of the cylinder, although very occasionally and in the more elaborate boxes they may be found in the center of the movement.

TABLE-TOP CYLINDER MUSIC BOXES Defining a table-top music box is rather like asking the length of a piece of string. However, some music boxes can be immediately discounted – those boxes that were built to be part of a complete item of furniture cannot be defined as table-top models. Interchangeable cylinder boxes that had a cabinet or drawers under them to store the cylinders, music boxes that were incorporated into writing desks, china cabinets, library tables, and so forth, and music boxes that were large enough to require a purpose-made table or stand cannot be defined as table-top models either.

LEFT **This lacquered singing-bird lapis lazuli box was made by Reuge in the mid-1980s. It is complemented by a Swiss quartz watch. When the start button is pressed the lid opens and the miniature bird, which is ¾in (2cm) high, springs up. It turns around, opens its beak, flaps its wings, wags its tail, and disappears. The piece was inspired by the intricate automata made by Pierre Jaquet Droz and his son Henri Louis in the 1770s.**

That said, however, table-top boxes come in a wide range of sizes. Small boxes, with cases of approximately 8 × 13in (20 × 33cm) and with cylinders ranging in length from 1½in (4cm) to 6in (15cm) and with a cylinder of less than 1in (2.5cm) in diameter, could play between two and six tunes. Many of these boxes do not include dancing, dolls, zither attachment or tune counters.

Larger boxes, ranging from 9 × 14 × 10in (23 × 36 × 25cm) to over 49 × 69 × 24in (125 × 175 × 61cm), could have cylinders ranging in length from 7in (17.5cm) to over 30in (76cm), and with diameters of 1in (2.5cm) to 4in (10cm). Such music boxes could play from six to twelve or more tunes.

These larger models came in a variety of cases, from the simple to the elegant. Many different techniques were employed in their decoration, some having fine inlaid patterns of wood or brass. Some were decorated with decals, while others simply had highly polished and veneered finishes.

FLOOR-STANDING CYLINDER MUSIC BOXES Although the cylinder music box was produced for a much longer time than the disc music box, comparatively few were made as floor-standing models. Most cylinder boxes were regarded as table models, although the size of some of the larger ones required custom-built tables or cabinets, and, as we have seen, some mechanisms were built into self-contained items of furniture. Nicole Frères, for example, made a writing desk model overture box, which contained a cylinder 19in (48cm) long and had storage space for 10 cylinders.

Many interchangeable cylinder music boxes were housed in immensely ornate cabinets, but floor models of the cylinder mechanism were usually gambling devices, which were very popular between 1900 and 1920. Most of these units were produced by the Mills Novelty Co. of Chicago, Illinois, or by

Caille Brothers of Detroit, Michigan. These machines might include roulette wheels, dice shakes, or mechanical horse races.

Other floor-standing cylinder music boxes included cases with glass fronts to enable a chirping bird to be seen, and some of these also contained cards bearing background scenes that were changed as the music played.

DISC MUSIC BOXES

These music boxes are instantly identifiable by the changeable disc. The cylinder and pin movement of the cylinder music box is replaced by an assembly consisting of a series of star-shaped wheels (known as star wheels), which are mounted on shaft. The

BELOW A contemporary Thorens 11in (28cm) disc **player in an elegantly styled inlaid case with a glass front.**

action of the shaft is the equivalent of the turning cylinder. The pins of the cylinder are replaced by projections on the lower side of the disc, although on some discs the points of the star projected through slots. As the disc revolves, the star wheels are turned and pluck the teeth of the comb to produce the notes. To change the tune, the disc is simply changed by placing the hole in the center of the disc over a spindle in the center of the box.

The cases of boxes made in Europe were mostly finished with walnut-veneer oak, although some mahogany or oak cases were also produced. Most boxes made in the United States were of mahogany or oak; a few had walnut or cherry inlay or veneer.

DAMPERS Dampers for disc boxes serve the same purpose as the dampers in a cylinder box. The difference is that these are usually more complex. They are usually easy to see once the disc has been removed, and they should be clearly visible between the tips of each tooth of the comb. Dampers were made from a variety of materials, ranging from felt, catgut and cam levers to slender friction wires. Different manufacturers used different methods. One of Lochmann's early systems, for example, used a comb with thin, felt-covered metal teeth, which was mounted under the musical comb; as the star wheel turned its first action was to press the damper teeth against the musical teeth. The system was not long lived.

RIGHT **The side and front view of a large Regina automatic changer, which was made as a floor-standing model. It was made around 1902 for home use and took 27in (68.5cm) discs. There are two spring motors: one for the musical movement and one to operate the changer. The round knob is the disc selector control. Around the outside edge of this knob are the numbers 1–12, to indicate which disc was to be selected. The discs sit in a carriage that is housed below that movement and can slide back and forth under it. When the knob is turned, the carriage is moved so that it aligns in such a way that the correct disc is played.**

LEFT **The Polyphon Casket model with a disc in playing position.**

DISC The changeable, record-type discs were usually made of metal, and they held the tune arrangement that activates the musical mechanism. One of the more noticeable features of the disc music box is the slots that can be seen on the upper surface of the discs. Punching a small slot on the top of the disc caused projections or prongs to protrude on the lower surface, and it is these projections that turn the star wheel.

DISHING ROLLERS These rollers are mounted opposite each other on either side of the inside of the case. When the disc is placed over the spindle and star wheels, the outer edge of the disc rides on these rollers. Because they are higher than the mechanism, they cause the disc to bow or dish, which ensures that the projections or slots are in contact with the star wheels. A pressure bar or pressure arm, which is a bar with rollers, closes over the disc to hold it in place over the star wheels. This action, combined with the dishing rollers, helps to keep the disc in a bowed or dish shape.

DRIVE MECHANISM Disc music boxes have two main types of mechanism – center drive and peripheral drive.

In center-drive music boxes the spring motor is connected to the center spindle and one, two or three pins (depending on the manufacturer), which were placed near to the spindle. The disc has holes at the center that fit over the spindle and pin(s). When the mechanism is turned on, the disc is turned by the drive action from the center pin or pins.

In peripheral-drive mechanisms the spring motor is connected to a sprocket that is located at the outer edge of the mechanism. The outer edge of the disc contains a series of holes that match the sprocket. The disc is placed over a fixed center spindle, with its outer edge placed over or into the projections of the sprocket. As the mechanism operates, the disc is turned by the drive action of the turning sprocket.

ABOVE **Many types of drive mechanisms were employed to turn the discs. The contemporary (c. 1970) Thorens 11in (28cm)** Edelweiss model uses a center drive, which required two drive holes, one on either side of the center hole as can be seen here.

FLOOR-STANDING DISC MUSIC BOXES Disc music boxes seem to belong naturally in upright cases, and as the discs got larger, the mechanisms were increasingly housed in this kind of case. Some of the larger mechanisms were housed in horizontal cabinets, however, even though these were too large to be thought of as table-top models.

A good example of a floor-standing cabinet is the Stella Orchestral Grand. Stella disc boxes were made by Mermod Frères, and they used a projection-less disc. This model played a 26in (66cm) disc, and some versions were powered by electricity rather than being spring wound. These units were very large – one model was 33½ × 41 × 30in (85 × 104 × 76cm). Regina incorporated a unit in a library table, and marketed it as a lady's desk. With the top closed, this unit measured 40½ × 20 × 30¾in (103 × 51 × 78cm). Regina also made a curved, glass-fronted china cupboard, which incorporated a 15½ (39.5cm) disc changer. According to the company's records, 11 of these units were made in 1905–6.

The Stella model 202, which played 26in (66cm) discs, was built for home use – it was 6ft (1.8m) high and 3ft (90cm) deep – and the upper portion of the cabinet had two doors with glass inserts through which the mechanism could be viewed.

Among the better known upright floor models are several made by Regina. The 27in (68.5cm) Orchestral was the largest range that the company produced, with a height of 80in (2m). The first units, which appeared in 1896, had a single disc that had to be changed manually, but a duplex comb, with 86 notes on each comb covering a total of over seven octaves, was introduced in the Orchestral Corona.

The Reginaphone is probably the best known of several disc-playing music boxes that incorporated a means of adjusting the mechanism so that phonograph recordings could be played. The space

LEFT **A Polyphon 18½in (46.5cm) disc player in a floor-standing cabinet. When the lid is closed, the unit measures 41 × 27½ × 23in (104 × 70 × 58.5cm).**

RIGHT **This large floor-standing Imperial Symphonion disc player (c.1896) takes 27½in (70cm) discs. The unit is 85 × 39 × 22in (216 × 99 × 56cm), and features 12 bells that accompany the tune. The name Imperial Symphonion was used for models that were built in the United States, and these machines are virtually unknown in Europe. Access to the storage area for discs in the base of the unit is gained by tilting forwards the front panel, which is hinged at the bottom.**

under the bedplate was used as an acoustic box or amplifier, which served equally well for the phonograph record or the music box disc. Some models had a detachable horn, which was used when a phonograph record was played.

The units that included automatic disc changers tended to be large, simply because of the space required to store the discs. The Polyphon upright music box that played 22½in (57.5cm) discs had a rack in the bottom of the unit that held 10 different discs. A pointer on the front of the cabinet allowed the tune to be selected. These mechanisms often also included bells to accompany the music.

Regina's style 31, which was intended for home use, played 20¾in (53cm) discs. It was furnished with an on/off lever, and the automatic changer held 12 discs in a carriage located in the lower half of the unit. The case, which was available in oak or mahogany, measured 64 × 34 × 24in (163 × 83 × 61cm).

The Regina Corona, which played 15½in (39.5cm) discs, was an automatic-change machine. The 12 discs were located in a carriage in the lower part of the unit, and all 12 tunes could be played twice on a single winding, each disc being replaced in its original position in the carriage after it had finished playing.

The style 35 Corona had a cabinet that was designed to look like a hall table with Queen Anne style legs. The upper portion of the unit had glass doors and an ornately molded cornice.

Symphonion, too, made some large and impressive pieces. The company's style 100 held 12 21½in (54.5cm) discs, which could be selected by turning a crank on the front. The music was accompanied by 10 bells. Another tall, elegant model, which played 25¼in (64cm) discs, had two combs with a total of 192 teeth. The mechanism would play for about 18 minutes on a single winding.

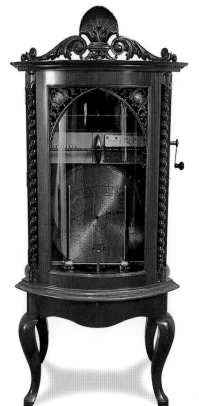

RIGHT **A Regina 15½in (39.5cm) automatic changer with its door open and shut. The discs may be seen resting in their carriage at the bottom of the unit. The unit holds 12 discs, and these are selected by turning a knob in the side of the cabinet. The knob moves the carriage to the correct position so that the selected disc can be picked up and played on the mechanism. Note the picture mounted on the back of the case.**

NOVELTY MUSIC BOXES

CHAPTER 4

The range of music boxes that is available seems to be almost endless, and the more you look into the subject the wider the range will become. Some collectors specialize in novelty boxes, and within that field, it is possible to specialize still further.

During the 19th century, for example, musical mechanisms were included in items as diverse as footstools, trivets, kitchen utensils, Christmas tree stands, lamps, humidors, cigarette cases, opera glasses and stereopticons. Photograph albums with musical movements were very popular from *c.*1880 to the end of the century; the mechanism was wound by a key or pull string, and the music played when the album was opened.

Swiss chalet jewelry boxes seem to have been perennially popular subjects for musical movements, and many are still being made. Other, more recent examples of items containing mechanical movements are note pad holders, beer cans, dust pans, watering cans, Christmas ornaments, greetings cards, and even bathroom fixtures. If you are prepared to extend your definition of music box to include electronically powered or battery-operated items, you might find yourself acquiring birthday candles, ceramic drinking mugs (these are operated by light-sensitive pads), and even a fly swatter.

An article in *The Music Trade Review* dated January 1902 described a "musical staircase" – this

LEFT AND ABOVE **The photograph album, which dates from the 1920s, is mounted on a wood base, which houses a two-tune musical movement. When the last page is turned, the movement may be seen through the celluloid window.**

had been devised to play tunes as you walked up and down stairs. The musical staircase is rather extreme, and you would probably have to move house to find the space to keep it. Other items are easy to accommodate, however.

FURNITURE

As we have seen, many of the leading makers placed musical mechanisms in articles of furniture. Among the most popular were full-size decorative tables, with a compartment to store stationery or playing cards, and smaller tea or serving tables. The problem facing the collector of music boxes is that these items are rarely obviously fitted with a musical mechanism, and they may well be passed over.

A child's rocking chair was made with a musical mechanism mounted on the rocker; each time the plunger was pushed a note would be played. Some wooden chairs had musical movements installed; the mechanism was operated by a hinged seat, so that when someone sat down, the on/off trigger was pressed.

ABOVE **A musical table dating from** *c.*1940. **This large octagonal table is finished with an inlaid floral design set in a light background. The divided storage area, often used to hold stationery or cards, is visible.**

BELOW **A modern version of an occasional table with a music box. The piece is decorated with a simple** inlaid design and finished with a high gloss, and the lid can be opened to reveal a Reuge 18-note movement.

BELOW **A child's musical rocking chair dating from** *c.*1940. **The movement is beneath the red metal cover. The movement of the rocking causes a plunger, which passes through the rocker and protrudes on the underside, to turn the cylinder.**

RIGHT **This liquor decanter in the form of a golf bag dates from c.1940 and plays an 18-note movement, which is activated when the decanter is raised. It has a metal handle and brass cylinder for the center section, which is trimmed with leather bands at the top and bottom.**

ABOVE AND LEFT **This early 1990s musical rocking chair has a spring-wound mechanism located in a plastic housing that is mounted on the rocker. A plunger extends from the side of the housing and protrudes beneath the rocker. As the child rocks, the plunger winds the spring. The tune continues to play for a while even when the rocking ceases.**

HOUSEHOLD UTENSILS

Many candy or serving dishes have been made with musical movements mounted in the lid or the base. Elegant teapots in the traditional style and novelty teapots have been made over the years. Designs have included Victorian houses, cats, and, recently, a cow. The mechanisms in items such as teapots are either played by winding the music and letting it play down or by an on/off trigger that allows the music to play only when the teapot is lifted. Lazy Susans (revolving trays that can be placed in the center of a dining table so that people can help themselves) have been made as simple molded units with 18-note movements, and as grand hand-crafted pieces made of metal and containing three-tune, 72-note mechanisms.

Musical liquor decanters are available in numerous styles and shapes, ranging from golf bags to cars. There are even some based on famous people – one decanter is in the form of Elvis Presley, and a musical movement is mounted in the base!

CLOCKS AND WATCHES

Many table clocks were made with good musical movements, but it can be difficult to identify musical clocks when you come across them in antique or second-hand stores because the musical mechanisms are not working. Often this is only because the mechanisms need cleaning and oiling, which is a straightforward and inexpensive repair.

Many of the makers of disc music boxes incorporated their mechanisms into hall clocks.

ABOVE **A 4½in (11cm) Thorens disc player in an upright, clock-style case, c.1980. The disc is of black-finish steel and the mechanism has a gold electroplated finish. The drive gear on this model is** located at the base of the winding key. The disc drive mechanism is actually a gear that meshes with the saw-toothed outer edge of the disc and turns it in order that the tune may be played.

Polyphon, for example, made a 14-day pendulum clock with a double comb and 11¼in (28.5cm) disc, which played on the hour. The clock was 92 × 24 × 15in (234 × 61 × 38cm). Another Polyphon mechanism, this time playing a 15½in (39.5cm) disc, was housed in a clock measuring 110 × 28 × 14in (280 × 71 × 36cm).

Symphonion's model 36B/106, which played 19⅛in (48.5cm) discs, was an elegant cabinet that contained the disc player and a grandfather clock. The disc movement had two combs and a total of 106 notes. The cabinet was 106 × 25½ × 17in (270 × 65 × 43cm). The Eroica, Symphonion's model 38A, played three 14in (36cm) disks simultaneously on three separate pairs of combs (that is, six combs in all), with a total of 300 teeth. The whole mechanism was housed with a clock in a tall, ornate case measuring 108 × 28½ × 17in (275 × 72 × 43cm).

Musical movements can also be found in cuckoo clocks, decorative pieces for the mantel piece and so forth.

From the first, cylinder music boxes have been incorporated into pocket watches and pocket watch cases. Early examples are rare and valuable. However, modern pocket watches with musical movements, some with animated pictures on the face, are now being made. They range in price from $15,000 downwards.

AUTOMATA

The finest automata were made in and around Paris in the latter half of the 19th century, where manufacturers such as Théroude, Decamps, Lambert, and Vichy relied on the skills of hundreds of outworkers. The musical movements, however, were often Swiss-made. These movements were concealed in a landscape base or, sometimes, in the body of the automaton. The mechanisms had very elaborate sets of cams and gears to allow the automaton to perform, and because the spring motor for these pieces was rather large, the musical mechanism often did not have its own spring motor but was simply driven from a geared take-off of the main spring motor.

Among the figures that were made were dolls, monkeys, jesters and children doing all manner of complicated things. Vichy, for example, made the figure of a smoker, with a Negro head, whose glass eyes look up and down while the figure rocks in a chair and smokes a pipe. Smoke from the pipe is

ABOVE **This modern reproduction of a turn-of-the-century ferris wheel is 14in (36cm) high, and it is one of a series of animated musical collectibles made by the Enesco Corporation in the** **Small World of.Music series. This piece is more of an automaton than a music box, and the multi-colored lights, music, intricate details, and craftsmanship make it a collectible.**

ABOVE **Enesco made this gazebo in the early 1990s. As the music plays, the floor revolves and the couple turn backwards and forwards as if dancing. The lights in the three lanterns and the** **movement of the dancers are controlled, like the musical mechanism, by the on/off control at the side of the unit. The mechanical movement is key-wound from underneath.**

drawn through a hole in the middle finger of the Negro's right hand, down his arm and out of his mouth. While the figure sits and smokes, rocking in the chair, the musical movement plays two tunes.

Roullet & Decamps, another French company, made an extraordinary automaton of pierrot and the moon c.1890. The papier mâché moon has a painted face with fixed, brown glass eyes and a tongue, which moves from side to side. The pierrot meanwhile raises a leg and lifts one arm, making movements as if to play a guitar, while the key-wound mechanism plays a waltz.

Such pieces are rare and expensive. However, the popularity of automata persisted throughout the century, and less complex items can be found. Birds in cages and birds that moved from branch to branch of a tree were great favorites, and were often accompanied by a clock. These pieces were a speciality of Charles Bontems of Paris. Pictures, parts of which moved, were especially popular in Victorian Britain, and many have survived. They were often combined with a small clock set in a church tower, and many were night scenes, illuminated by mother of pearl "moonlight".

MODERN COLLECTIBLES

Several modern companies are producing unusual musical boxes. Enesco's Small World of Music Collection has 150 unusual items, of which two of the most interesting are Toyland and Treasure Chest of Toys. These and other items in Enesco's output may be candidates for long-term collections.

One music box currently available is a kaleidoscope that is mounted on a wooden base. The top of the base also has a disc mounted on it. The disc, which contains various pieces of stained glass and reflective baubles, is mounted so that it revolves around a central spindle. The musical movement is connected to the disc, and when the spring is wound the tune is played and the disc rotates under the barrel of the tube holding the lenses and mirrors.

Many types of small carousel are available. Most have musical movements that both play the tune and turn the carousel. There are usually four horses, and these may move up and down on a central pole.

ABOVE This curious music box, made in 1992, is in the form of an old-fashioned typewriter. It was produced by Enesco in its Small World of Music series. Two figures move across the clicking keys, while a third figure staples papers as the space bar moves up and down and the paper moves conti- nuously around the platen. The box plays "Whistle While You Work" on an 18-note movement, which is powered by a small electric motor.

ABOVE This early 1990s child's music box was produced by Enesco.

ABOVE An Enesco box, housing an 18- note movement.

ABOVE This contemporary carousel contains an 18-note Sankyo movement.

NOVELTY MUSIC BOXES

The number of novelty items that have musical movements is breathtaking. If this is the area that interests you, you might want to consider limiting your acquisitions to a specific area. Listed here are some of the subjects – but the choice is yours.

Airplanes and aviation	Football
Alarm clocks (travel and wall-mounted ones)	Frogs
	Geese
Animals	Globes
Automobiles/cars	Golf
Baby items	Gramophones/phonographs
Ballerinas	Harps
Banks	Horses
Baseball	Hot-air balloons
Basketball	Hunting
Bears	Jewelry boxes
Beer steins	Keepsake boxes
Bells	Key chains
Birds	Madonnas
Bridal items	Mice
Butterflies	Music and musical
Cable cars	instruments
Cardinals	Nurses
Carousels	Nutcrackers
Castles	Photograph frames/albums
Cats	Pianos
Children's music boxes	Religious items
Christmas ornaments and items	School
	Smokers
Churches	Spinning tops
Clocks	Swiss chalets
Clowns	Taverns
Delft	Teachers
Disneyana	Teapots
Dogs	Tennis
Dolls	Tigers
Dragons	Trains
Ducks	Turtles
Elephants	Unicorns
Fairy-tale items	Victoriana
Fish	Windmills
Flowers	Wizards

ABOVE Made in the early 1990s, this collectible by Steinbach represents Mozart at the piano. The 18-note movement inside the piano plays "Tristesse". The pull-type on/off control is located on the side of the piano.

BELOW The Smoking Fisherman by Steinbach was made in the mid-1980s. An 18-note Reuge movement plays the tune and powers the movement. When the tune plays, the boat rocks from side to side as it travels forwards. The incense burner plate is revealed by removing the figure of the fisherman.

LEFT **The Rocking Chair smoker by Steinbach, made in the mid-1980s, has an 18-note Swiss musical movement that powers the rocking motion and plays the tune. On the right-hand side of the chair is the wooden knob that activates the mechanism by means of an on/off pull pin.**

RIGHT **The Smoking Man was made by Steinbach in the mid-1980s and is regarded as a collectible in its own right. The body lifts off to permit access to a metal plate that is used as an incense burner. This figure represents the *Oktoberfest*. A single-tune, 18-note (1/18) Reuge movement is mounted in the drum on the figure's back.**

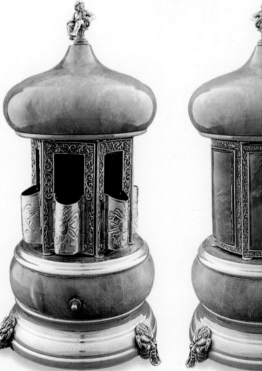

LEFT **This 1980s German beer stein contains an 18-note Swiss movement activated by a spring-loaded on/off pin, which is released when the stein is raised.**

RIGHT **This 1950s mosque houses a cylinder with a 36-note movement by Thorens. The large diameter of the cylinder allows two long tunes to be played by a single revolution of the cylinder. When the button is pushed the doors in the center begin to open. The first tune plays until the inside panels of the doors are fully exposed; the second tune plays while the doors swing round until they are in their original position.**

CARING FOR YOUR ACQUISITIONS

CHAPTER 5

The first rule of maintenance and the one you will hear from craftsmen who repair music boxes is: if it works, don't fix it.

One of the most wonderful aspects of owning a music box is that you do not have to do very much to maintain it in working order. Provided that it is handled with reasonable care – that it is not dropped or set down too hard – the major problem will be the accumulation of dirt in the bearing and pivot points, which will cause excess friction and slow down or bind the movement.

CLEANING AND OILING

If you acquire a music box and find that the music does not play or is playing too slowly, you can carry out minor cleaning and oiling of the governor mechanism yourself. You do not have to disassemble the governor fully to perform this task. The primary problem is probably normal wear and tear, and you must clean the mechanism before you oil it, or very soon the mechanism will grind to a complete halt.

The cleaning process described here depends on the use of a good solvent and a stream of compressed air. It is carried out with the governor mounted firmly in place.

You will need good clock oil, some good solvent, and a cotton swab or a toothpick and a small swatch of cloth. Do not use brushed cotton or lint, otherwise small pieces will adhere to the mechanism. Do not use any silicone-type spray lubricants that are available in some stores. Do not use cleaning solvents that have aromatic ingredients or that leave a residue.

Find a clock manufacturer or clock repair shop where you can obtain a pin point oiler and some good quality clock oil. Some companies make disposable

LEFT **This classic phonograph-style case, complete with brass horn, houses a 4½in (11cm)** **Thorens disc player. A crank lever is used instead of the traditional winged winding key.**

RIGHT **The small case houses a cylinder mechanism made by Lador, *c.*1880; it has been disassembled. In front of the case and to the left is the bedplate and to the right are the comb and cylinder. On the left of the cylinder is the great wheel (large gear), which is still mounted on the shaft that passes through the cylinder. On the right-hand** side of the cylinder are the spring housing, governor assembly, mounting screws, and winding key. The unit is wound by key from the bottom. The key itself is not threaded; instead, it has a square opening on the bottom, resembling the type of key used to wind a clock.

oilers, ready filled with clock oil, and these are relatively cheap and contain sufficient oil for a hundred or more governor mechanisms.

Some good solvents are available in aerosol cans. If you choose this kind, make sure that it has a long, flexible extension tube. This will enable you to apply the solvent directly into the point you need. Remember, never use silicone or aromatic solvents. Again, clock repairers, clock manufacturers, or even an electronics components supplier would be a possible source. Alternatively, you could use a clean solvent such as lacquer thinner and a canister of compressed air, which you will probably find in an art supply or hobby store because compressed air is often used with air brushes. Electronic components suppliers might also be able to provide the aerosol canisters that are used in the cleaning of computers and computer keyboards. Again, you must make sure that you have an extended, flexible nozzle or adaptor so that you can apply the solvent precisely where you need it. Whichever kind of solvent you use, you will have to repeat the cleaning process several times. Allow time between applications for the solvent to work.

First, locate the governor mechanism. Then examine the worm and pivots for lint, threads, hair, and so on, and remove these with tweezers. Next clean the pivot (bearing) points. These are the points where the endless screw is inserted into the top bracket and the bottom plate. In older boxes the top of the endless screw is located under a jewel. The other points will be found at either end of the shafts that hold a gear in place. These mounting holes will be located in the sides of the governor housing.

Before you begin, protect the rest of the mechanism from the solvent spray. If any of the solvent gets onto the other parts of the mechanism it may leave spots or, worse, remove the protective coatings. You could use stiff plastic or cardboard; do not use cloth or anything that might get caught on the cylinder pins or in the gearing. If the mechanism should accidentally begin to work, these materials can easily get jammed in the gearing, wrapped around the cylinder or even caught between the cylinder and the teeth, which would be disastrous.

Without removing the governor assembly, direct the pin point extension tube at each of the points. If you are using an aerosol-charged solvent you will be applying solvent and using its pressure to both soften and remove the dirt. The first pass is to clear any loose particles of dust or dirt from the points. Repeat the process as often as necessary. Alternatively, apply the solvent to these points with an applicator such as a toothpick. Apply only one or two drops of solvent to each point. Leave the solvent to work, then use a canister of plain compressed air to remove the dirt. Apply a second coat of solvent, and repeat the process as often as necessary.

Before oiling the mechanism, allow time for all of the solvent to dry thoroughly, then, without removing the governor assembly, put a drop of oil on the points. Remember: if you are using a pin point oiler you have enough oil to apply to more than a hundred governors. You need only a very small amount. As you apply it, you will see that the oil spreads on the surface around the point. Wipe off this excess oil with a cotton swab or a small piece of cloth on a toothpick. It is important to wipe away all excess oil because it is oil that attracts dust and dirt.

Major cleaning and oiling of the governor, which involves cleaning and polishing the components (spring, motor, cranks and levers, cylinder) and cleaning and painting the bedplate, is best done by a specialist repairer, and restoration, should it be required, is always best carried out by a skilled craftsman. A complete overhaul involves checking the bushing, bearings, shafts, pivot points, spring and spring motor assembly, gears, cylinder, pins and comb for wear and tolerance, and it requires the complete disassembly of all the components of the movement. All the items are checked for wear that might cause misalignment or looseness, and are repaired as necessary. The spring is inspected, cleaned and greased. All visible parts are cleaned and polished and a cast iron bedplate repainted, before being oiled and re-assembled. Such a restoration would also include dampering the teeth and re-tuning if necessary.

MOVING AND STORING MUSIC BOXES

You may sometimes have to move or store a music box, and there are several steps you must take to protect it.

First, before you move it more than a short distance, allow it to play down so that the spring is unwound. Make sure that when the spring is unwound the cylinder has stopped so that the tips of the teeth are positioned in the blank area of the cylinder. If the cylinder pins are in contact with any of the teeth for any length of time, the teeth will eventually remain in that position.

If you have to store a music box for any length of time, allow the spring to unwind as above, and then pack it as if you were going to send it on a long sea journey. Mark the container clearly, and store it in a safe place with average humidity and a moderate temperature range.

BELOW A Swiss chalet, made c.1989 by Adrion Taron, with an 18-note Swiss movement that is wound from the bottom. When the top is lifted, it plays "Holiday in Switzerland".

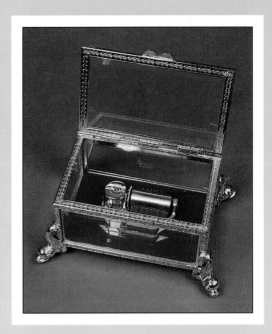

COLLECTING MUSIC BOXES

CHAPTER 6

A useful rule of thumb when you are thinking of buying a music box is that expensive movements are never found in cheap cases.

Collecting music boxes should be a labour of love. Look upon the time and money you spend as a long-term investment. Although you should not regard the acquisition of a music box as a financial investment, there is no doubt that, with the steady and growing demand for a limited number of pre-World War I boxes, the music boxes available today offer a wide range of items that should have lasting and increasing value.

ANTIQUE MUSIC BOXES

Music boxes made before World War I may be considered as antiques. There is a tremendous range to choose from, covering a wide range of prices. This category includes the very old, extremely rare pieces made in the early years of music box development to the popular examples that were built towards the end of the period. You will find everything from snuff-boxes and pocket watches, through spring-wound cartel boxes to hand-cranked, manivelle-type music boxes. Prices may range from less than $50 (£35.00) to many thousands of dollars.

One of the most enjoyable aspects of collecting the older music boxes is that there are many fellow collectors and craftsmen who will be able to assist with maintenance, repairs and restoration.

If you are buying a classic or antique music box, look out for good movements and cases. If these are treated with reasonable care and given regular maintenance, and you will have a desirable and valued collection.

LEFT **This contemporary crystal box with brass trimmings, dolphin-style brass feet, and a hinged lid,** **contains a single-tune, 36-note (1/36) Reuge movement, which is activated and wound from underneath.**

TRADITIONAL MUSIC BOXES

This category includes music boxes that have been made since *c.*1900, and it includes many of the finer disc-playing boxes. The better movements will have between 28 and 144 notes, compared with the cheaper models, which have between 12 and 18 notes. Many of these boxes have been stored away and forgotten about, and are only now being passed on to the next generation. There seems to be a fair number of these boxes on the market at the moment, but demand is growing and supplies are limited.

ABOVE This three-tune, 72-note (3/72) movement by Reuge is mounted in an inlaid music box, the elegant and simple lines of which are reminiscent of the shape and styling of the fine cases that were used with cartel boxes in the latter part of the 19th century. This box was made around 1988 – the case and assembly were completed by Ed Jobin Ag. The outer edges of the lid are shaped and finished in high-gloss black. When the lid is opened, two lined side compartments and the central compartment, which houses a Reuge movement, are revealed. The center compartment is covered with a hinged glass lid that emulates the earlier style. There are brass handles at the side of the case, and a mirror is mounted on the inside of the lid. The on/off control is operated by the small brass button in the center of the front panel.

LEFT **An inlaid case by Reuge for its key-wound three-tune sublime harmonie movement. The burr walnut case is inlaid with tulip wood lines, and the musical instruments are formed from 56 pieces of tinted sycamore and mahogany. The case is 16¾ × 7½ × 4in (42.5 × 19 × 10cm).**

NEW MUSIC BOXES

The music boxes that are being made today are, of course, easier to acquire, and some of the better makers are producing pieces that will become the collector's items of tomorrow.

REUGE CO. This Swiss company offers a wide range of excellent music boxes. The list includes a baby's stuffed animal with an 18-note movement operated by a pull ring and, at the other end of the scale, an interchangeable mechanism with five cylinders with four tunes on each cylinder and a sublime harmonie movement with 144 notes, operated by a crank wind. The highly polished case includes a storage drawer for the extra cylinders. Another music box, offered in a rosewood box, in a burr walnut and rosewood inlaid box, or in a clock that strikes the hour and plays one tune, has a sublime harmonie movement with a double comb composed of 144 teeth, which plays four tunes over five octaves and has a total running time of 15 minutes. It has a ratchet lever.

LEFT **A Reuge four-tune cartel movement mounted in an ornate crystal box. The unit is wound by a ratchet lever, which is located at the left-hand side, and is activated by an on/off lever at the right-hand side of the movement. A tune counter is mounted at the rear, behind the cylinder. Both the spring barrel and cylinder are mounted horizontally, and the spring is wound from the side of the mechanism.**

Reuge's products range from $20 (£15.00) to over $70,000 (£50,000). At the top end of its range it recently made a limited edition of a revolver cartel box with six cylinders with four tunes on each. In its catalog it lists chalets and musical bells; jewelry boxes with inlay designs; traditional music boxes with cases ranging from plain wood to intricately inlaid patterns; pocket watches, with 17-note or 35-note changing movements; musical automata; and disc music boxes playing 4½in (11cm) and 11in (28cm).

The company's policy is now not to sell musical movements bearing the Reuge name to other companies for inclusion in non-Reuge cases. All Reuge musical movements will be installed in Reuge-made cases and sold through the company's own sales organization. This means that in future, Reuge products are likely to be at the top of the price range. However, still on the market are Reuge movements in other companies' cases; an astute collector will look out for these boxes, which will inevitably appreciate in value.

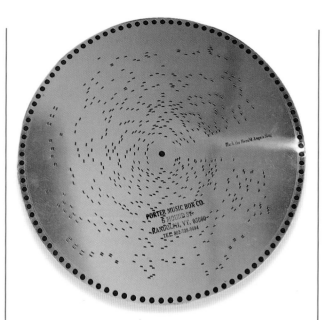

ABOVE **This 15½in (39.5cm) disc, which was made by Porter, of Randolph, New York, will play on Regina,** **Polyphon or Porter machines that take 15½in (39.5cm) discs.**

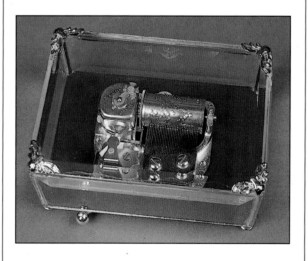

ABOVE **The single-tune, 30-note (1/30) Sankyo movement, dating from the early 1990s, is contained in a sealed case of beveled glass. The mechanism is activated by a lever that is mounted** **under the case and that extends to the front edge of the case for easy access. The knob of the lever is visible in the lower left-hand corner of the box.**

PORTER MUSIC BOX CO. This American company, which is based in Randolph, Vermont, has been producing disc music boxes since 1974. More than 750 boxes have been produced so far, and approximately 80 are made each year.

The 15½in (39.5cm) disc music box movements are modeled on the double-comb Regina box, and this means that the original Regina 15½in (39.5cm) discs can be played on it, and, conversely, Porter's discs can be played on the Regina box. Each comb has 76 teeth, and the motor will play for approximately 20 minutes on a single winding.

Porter offers several models, including table and upright versions, and some floor models. The Victorian Baroque Limited Edition is a table model, measuring 24 × 22 × 12in (61 × 56 × 30cm). The Twin Disc music box has an inlaid design on the cabinet, which is styled as a hall table, with four curved, Queen Anne style legs. It measures 30 × 22 × 42in (76 × 56 × 106cm), and there are four combs playing a total of 304 lengths on two synchronized disc units.

RIGHT **The inlaid case was made in Sorrento, Italy, in the 1980s. The floral design is set in a burlwood background. The case, which houses a Sankyo bee and bell movement, is 8 × 5 × 1¾in (20 × 12.5 × 4.5cm). It has two combs, with 22 teeth on each, a set of six bells with bee strikers, and a cylinder that is 2¾in (7cm) long. Weber's "Invitation to the Dance" is accented by bell accompaniment. The bells are played by a striker mechanism that is activated by attachments mounted to the underside of six teeth. These teeth are located at the outside edges of the comb set – three on each side – and these teeth are played by projections on the cylinder. As they are lifted, the striker mechanism causes the bees to strike the appropriate bells.**

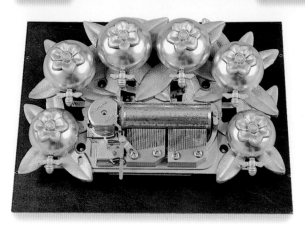

SANKYO This Japanese company has made several interesting musical movements. A two-tune, 50-note movement has a very good sound, although it is available in only a limited number of tunes. The cylinder shifts to play each tune, and the diameter of the cylinder is larger than comparable mechanisms made in Switzerland. The spring motor is built with a Geneva stop at the top of the spring barrel.

Another interesting Sankyo movement is a single-tune, 30-note mechanism. The tune selection is somewhat limited but the sound is good. Again, the spring motor has a Geneva stop on the top of the spring barrel.

Sankyo's bee and bell mechanism consists of a movement with two 22-note combs and a cylinder that is 2½in (7cm) long. Around the upper portion of the comb and cylinder, six bells have been attached to the bedplate. The strikers are shaped like bees, and as the tune plays, the striking of the bells emphasizes the rhythm.

SORRENTO SPECIALITIES LTD. This company has produced a 15½in (39.5cm) disc player, the units of which were finished with ornate inlay designs. It has also made several different table models and an upright unit. These machines are based on the original Regina 15½in (39.5cm) disc music boxes.

EXAMINING MUSIC BOXES

Before you handle or attempt to play or wind a music box, it is both courteous and prudent to ask permission. Allow the owner to demonstrate the box to you – there may be a problem that the owner is unaware of, and you could find yourself in an embarrassing situation if you operate a box only to have it break in your hands.

Most traditional and antique music boxes have an on/off or start mechanism. When this is activated the music usually plays for as long as the mechanism is in the on position. After the first notes are played, the switch can be turned to the off position. Many better quality mechanisms are designed so that when they are turned off, the music continues to play to the end of a pre-determined cycle before it stops. Many newer or less expensive music boxes will either not have an on/off switch (they will play until the spring runs down) or they stop immediately the

LEFT **This three-tune, 72-note (3/72) movement, which is mounted in sealed mahogany frame with a beveled glass top, dates from c.1985. The musical movement, which was made by Thorens, is activated by an extended lever, which is mounted underneath the case but is reached from the front. When the knob in the lower left-hand corner is turned off, the mechanism will continue to the end of the tune it is playing.**

LEFT **The great wheel (large gear) still mounted to the cylinder arbor that runs through the center of the cylinder. Note the dark ring around the outer edge of the gear: this is a groove machined into the gear. The on/off mechanism is operated by a lever that rides in this groove. When it is turned to the off position, spring tension from the lever assembly causes the lever to enter a stop hole that is aligned with the end of the tune arrangement on the cylinder. This feature allows the tune to be played to the end of the arrangement.**

control mechanism is in the off position.

However the music stops, it is important that none of the teeth is raised – that is, no tooth should be in contact with any pin on the cylinder. If the movement is left in this position for any length of time, stress on the raised tooth may cause it to bend and it may become permanently bowed. If the music box plays to the end of the tune and the cylinder has stopped automatically, there should be a blank area, with no pins, across the length of the cylinder, and this should be under the teeth. If the cylinder does not stop in this position, it should be adjusted by a craftsman or clock maker. If the cylinder does not have this feature, allow it to play to the end, then turn the mechanism off. Again, all the teeth should be aligned in the blank area on the cylinder between the end and beginning of the tune.

THE CYLINDER First of all, check to see if any of the pins are bent, rusty or missing.

If the music box has a multi-tune cylinder or an interchangeable cylinder, the mechanism must be positioned so that the blank area on the cylinder is under the teeth before you attempt to remove it or check to see if the cylinder slides. Attempting to move the cylinder, even when it has stopped turning, when the teeth are not in this position can cause damage to both the pins and the teeth. Although it is possible to re-pin a cylinder, this is a costly and time-consuming task that has to be carried out by a craftsman.

THE COMB Look for the obvious first – are any of the teeth missing? Look closely at the tips of the teeth to see if they are the same length. The tips of small, pointed teeth may be missing. Again, it is possible to replace or repair teeth, and replacing a tip is less costly than having to replace an entire tooth. However, these are expensive operations.

THE GOVERNOR Make sure that the governor is in place. Older mechanisms often have a jewel on the point at which the shaft holds the butterfly wings. If the mechanism has been repaired, this will probably have been replaced by a hard piece of steel. (It is possible to replace the steel by a jewel if you are restoring the music box to its original condition.) New mechanisms will have a hardened piece of steel here.

If the box is not working and you cannot immediately see the problem, do not remove the governor until you are quite certain that the spring is fully unwound and has no tension. Never attempt to loosen or remove the governor or its components without first knowing that there is no tension in the spring. You could easily cause irreparable damage.

THE SPRING MOTOR The key or lever used to wind the spring should move relatively easily. Never use force if you meet with resistance. It could be that the spring is already fully wound and something else is stopping the mechanism from working. The problem may be dirt and congealed grease or it may be a jammed mechanism; it is probably better to ask a clock repairer or craftsman to examine the spring. If, when you wind a mechanism, you hear a popping sound and feel a loss of tension, or if you just seem to wind and wind and not get any tension, the spring is probably broken.

THE MUSIC When the machine is playing, listen for any notes that are obviously out of tune. Do there seem to be any gaps in the notes or parts of the tune? This could mean that pins are missing, bent or worn.

Next listen to the loudness of the sound to see if it is even while the cylinder turns. If the level of sound changes, it may be that the cylinder is not turning in a perfect circle or that some pins or teeth are badly worn.

Sometimes a music box may seem to be in tune and yet you can hear strange buzzing or scraping noises. If this is a good quality box with more than 18 notes, the dampers on the middle and bass notes may have become misaligned or broken, and this will cause these piercing noises. Dampers can usually be adjusted or replaced.

BELOW **This reproduction case has a section for keepsakes and an animated butterfly. The box has a beveled glass lid, with an etched floral pattern on the left-hand side. The felt-lined interior has a small compartment for keepsakes, while the right-hand side contains a single-tune, 18-note (1/18) musical movement. The butterfly flaps its wings when the lid is opened and the tune is played.**

BELOW **The single-tune, 36-note (1/36) romance movement is contained in an olive wood piano, $7\frac{1}{2} \times 6 \times 4\frac{1}{2}$in ($19 \times 15\frac{1}{2} \times 11$cm). It was made in the early 1990s. The movement is activated when the piano lid is raised, and the unit is key-wound from underneath.**

DISC
MUSIC BOXES

CHAPTER 7

The following are the main models of disc music box that collectors are likely to encounter. Further details of most manufacturers are listed in Chapter 8, although the history of the three major companies, Polyphon, Regina and Symphonion is discussed in Chapter 2.

ADLER
Made by Julius H. Zimmermann (*q.v.*).
Both the standard mechanism and a double-disc machine were produced. Disc sizes ranged from 7¼in (18cm) to 26in (66cm), and the machine was made in several models, both upright and horizontal.
Trademark: eagle in flight before a sunrise.

BASKANION
Made by Paul Ehrlich & Co. *(q.v.)* of Fabrik Leipziger Musikwerke, Leipzig, Germany, 1889. A card-style disc machine, with a disc size of 11¼in (28.5cm).

BRITANNIA
Made by B. H. Abrahams (*q.v.*). Disc sizes ranged from 5in (13cm) to 25in (63cm). The Britannia has a good, clear tone and was made in both upright and horizontal models. The Smoker's Cabinet is an upright machine that plays a 9in (23cm) steel disc. See also Imperial. Trademark: lion with a globe inside a sunburst.

LEFT **A 27½in (70cm) Regina disc made c. 1896, showing the trademark and the drive holes located at the outer edge.**

LEFT **The owner of these 20½in (52cm) Kalliope discs believes that one was produced for sale in the United States and the other for sale in Europe – the differences in printing style and layout designed to appeal to the separate markets.**

CAPITAL

Made by F. G. Otto (*q.v.*). The Capital Cuff Box, which was not a true disc music box, had a mechanism that was distinguished by its conical metal sleeve, which looked like an old-fashioned dress cuff. The sleeve was placed over a conical framework and turned like a cylinder music box. One model had a double-comb configuration. The cuffs ranged in size from 4½in (11cm) to 7¾in (20cm) in length.

CELESTA

Made by Pietschmann & Son (*q.v.*). These disc boxes are noted for the colorfully decorated discs, which ranged in size from 8½in (22cm) to 19⅝in (50.5cm). They were made in both upright and horizontal models, and the upright versions tend to have an image on the door of the cabinet rather than a glass panel. Trademark: *Celesta* in a scroll on a bed of flowers on the discs.

CELESTE

Made by Otto Helbig & Polikeit.

CRITERION

Made by F. G. Otto (*q.v.*). These disc boxes were made along the lines of the traditional interchangeable disc box. Disc sizes ranged from 11½in (29cm) to 20½in (52cm). The discs were made of zinc.

EDELWEISS

Made by Hermann Thorens (*q.v.*). These machines had good, clear tones and, although they were made in several sizes, it seems they were all table-top models. Early models used discs without projections, and the discs, which were usually of zinc, had lozenge-shaped, peripheral-drive holes. The discs ranged from 12in (30cm) to 22¼in (56.5cm). This model was also offered under the name Helvetia.

EMPRESS

Made by Mermod Frères (*q.v.*). This machine, which was identical to the Mira (*q.v.*), was made under this name for export by Lyon & Healy of Chicago, USA.

EROICA

Made by Symphonion (*q.v.*). A multiple-disc mechanism, it was made in two- or three-disc playing systems. The set of discs for this unit played simultaneously.

EUPHONIA

Made by F. G. Otto (*q.v.*). A later version of the Criterion (*q.v.*).

EUPHONION

Sold by Euphonion Musikwerke, Vienna, Austria. Disc sizes ranged from 11in (28cm) to 19⅝in (50.5cm), and the discs are interchangeable with Polyphon discs of the same size.

EUTERPEPHON

Made by A. W. Neumann (*q.v.*). Very few examples are extant. Trademark: center-drive discs have a lyre with a banner bearing the inscription *Euterpephon*.

FORTUNA

Made by Julius H. Zimmermann (*q.v.*). Zimmermann took over the Adler products and changed the name to

Fortuna. The Fortuna range included both upright and horizontal models. Trademark: eagle with spread wings holding in its beak a ribbon with the word *Patented* on it, with *Schutzmark* above and *Trade Mark* below.

GLORIA

Made by Société Anonyme (*q.v.*). These were available in both upright and horizontal models and used standard discs and combs. There were two disc sizes – 11¾in (30cm) and 18¼in (46cm). These disc music boxes should not be confused with the next model.

GLORIA

Made by Paul Ehrlich & Co. (*q.v.*). This twin-disc model played 26½in (67.5cm) discs.

HARMONIA

Made by Harmonia SA (*q.v.*). Discs, which did not have projections, ranged in size from 8in (20cm) to 16in (41cm).

HELVETIA

See Edelweiss.

IMPERATOR

Made by Friedrich Adolf Richter & Co. (*q.v.*). This model was made 1893–1900 and three versions have been identified: no. 27, which played a 5½in (14cm) disc, no. 52G, which played a 10¼in (26cm) disc, and no. 49, which played a 21in (53.5cm) disc. Trademark: *Imperator* in a circle around a flaming torch separating the words *Trade Mark* attached on a stamped medallion and cast on the bedplate.

IMPERIAL

See Britannia.

IMPERIAL SYMPHONION

Manufactured by Symphonion

Manufacturing Co., which was a branch of Symphonionfabrik Co. (*q.v.*).

JUNGHANS

Made by Junghanssche Uhrenfabrik (*q.v.*). Trademark: *J* within a star on the disc.

KALLIOPE

Made by Kalliope Musikwerke (*q.v.*). This model was made in both upright

and horizontal versions, some with bells. Some of the smaller models were wound through the spindle in the center of the mechanism. Disc sizes ranged from 5¾in (14.5cm) to 29½in (75cm).

KOMET

Made by Komet Musikwerke. The model was introduced by Franz Louis Bauer in 1894. There were two styles,

ABOVE **The Komet trademark of a man blowing** a horn appeared on the discs; this is a 21⅝in (54.5cm) disc.

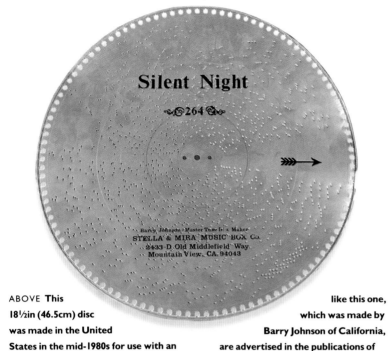

ABOVE **This 18½in (46.5cm) disc was made in the United States in the mid-1980s for use with an original Mira disc mechanism. Discs** like this one, **which was made by Barry Johnson of California, are advertised in the publications of the Musical Box Society International.**

the earlier using discs without projections. The discs were 13in (33cm), 17in (43cm), 21½in (54.5cm), and 33¼in (84.5cm), the last played on a huge upright machine with bell accompaniment.

LIBELLION

Made by Friedrich Adolf Richter & Co. (*q.v.*). This music box used a unique system of folding cardboard strips (music books).

LOCHMANN-ORIGINAL

Made by Paul Lochmann (*q.v.*). The discs for these boxes were made with a lipped edge and ranged in size from 5⅛in (13.5cm) to 29in (73.5cm). The range included both upright and horizontal models, some of which had bells. The discs bore the name *Lochmann-Original* but are otherwise plain.

MIRA

Made by Mermod Frères (*q.v.*). This machine was also known as the Empress, under which name it was sold in the USA. It seems likely (but by no means certain) that the Mira was made in a horizontal form only. Most have good quality cases, sometimes decorated with inlay, and the tone is good. Disc sizes ranged from 4½in (11cm) to 18½in (46.5cm).

MONARCH

Made by American Music Box Co. (*q.v.*). This model used a 15½in (39.5cm) disc. Apart from the design of the drive system, these discs would play on a Regina of the same size.

MONOPOL

Made by Paul Ehrlich & Co. (*q.v.*). The design of the mechanism is similar to that of the Symphonion in that it has a two-star wheel and comb assembly, one mounted on either side of the center. The discs for these machines are interchangeable with

LEFT **The Polyphon trademark appears on all the company's discs.**

RIGHT **The large oak case houses a converted coin-operated 15½in (39.5cm) double-comb Regina disc player. There is a crank handle on the right-hand side. The coin action has been disabled, but part of the mechanism remains on the front of the case.**

those made for a Symphonion with the same size disc and the same configuration on the comb and star wheel assembly. It is possible that some, at least, of the Monopol mechanisms were manufactured by Symphonion. Disc sizes ranged from 5¼in (13.5cm) to 26in (66cm).

OLYMPIA

Made by F. G. Otto (*q.v.*). This was made in the same style as the interchangeable disc box.

ORPHEUS

Made by Ludwig & Wild (*q.v.*) from 1897. Two sizes of disc were available – 12in (30cm) and 28⅝in (72cm), and the cabinets were large and heavy, the biggest measuring 86 × 30 × 20in (218 × 76 × 51cm) and having a comb with 220 teeth. The disc drive holes are square.

PERFECTION

Made by Perfection Music Box Co. (*q.v.*). These horizontal machines, which were produced from 1898 to 1901, used a unique damper arrangement. The star wheels were constructed with felt which was placed between two thin, star-shaped plates. A problem was that the felt became easily worn and was costly to replace. The discs bear the name *The Perfection* in a scroll and they range in size from 10⅝in (27.5cm) to 15½in (39.5cm).

POLYHYMNIA

Two different companies used this name; however, neither appears to have made large quantities and few examples have survived.

POLYMNIA

Made by Société Anonyme (*q.v.*). This

was a later addition to the company's range of disc music boxes and was produced in 1902–04. The discs had projections that were made by raising the metal to form dimples.

POLYPHON

Made by Polyphon Musikwerke (*q.v.*). This is the most often found disc music box. Production began in 1895 and discs are comparatively easy to obtain. Both upright and horizontal models were made, and they ranged in size from small units that could be held in the hand to upright models that were over 8ft (2.4m) high. The discs, all of which carried the name *Polyphon* and the company trademark, ranged in size from 6½in (16.5cm) to 24½in (62cm), with the 15½in (39.5cm) disc being the most popular.

Trademark: goddess/woman in flowing dress holding lyre and laurel wreath

below shooting star with *Polyphon* in the tail and above *Marque de Fabrique* in horseshoe-shaped cartouche printed on discs or stamped on round medallions on the case itself.

REGINA

Made by Regina Music Box Co. (*q.v.*). Some 100,000 disc music boxes were made during the life of the company. With a few exceptions, Regina discs of the same size are interchangeable with the Polyphon. Disc sizes ranged from less than 8½in (22cm) to 27in (68.5cm).
Trademark: lyre with intertwined branch of garland between two scrolled banners, one across the center of the lyre with the name *Regina* and the other, below the lyre, with the words *Trade Mark*.

SILVANIGRA

A series of small music boxes.

SIRION

Believed to have been made by G. Bortmann & A. Kelier (*q.v.*). These machines were made in only limited numbers and for a short time –

1895–1901 – and they are rare. They are also unusual in that each disc plays two tunes. Both horizontal and upright versions were produced.

STELLA

Made by Mermod Frères (*q.v.*). The unique design of the Stella makes these music boxes easy to identify. The discs for these machines did not have projections. Instead, the unit was designed so that the pressure arm goes completely across the disc. Disc sizes ranged from 9½in (24cm) to 26in (66cm).
Trademark: a cross with *S* within a five-pointed star above *Swiss*.

STERLING

Made by F. G. Otto (*q.v.*). A development of the Criterion.

SUN

Made by Schrämli & Tschudin (*q.v.*).

SYMPHONION

Made by Paul Lochmann (*q.v.*). The design of the mechanism is similar to that of the Monopol in that it has a two-star wheel and comb assembly, one mounted on either side of the center.

The discs for these machines are interchangeable with those of the Monopol, provided they are the same size and provided that the machine has the same configuration of the comb and star wheel assembly. There were at least 21 different disc sizes, ranging from 4½in (11cm) to 30in (76cm). Trademark: lyre with a banner across the front with *Symphonion* across it.

TANNHÄUSER

Made by Tannhäuser Musikwerke (*q.v.*). This very rare type of shifting disc was patented in 1897 and production began in Germany in 1899 but appears to have ceased in the following year.

TRIUMPH

Made by the American Music Box Co. (*q.v.*). This unit had a disc size of 15½in (39.5cm).

TROUBADOUR

Made by B. Grosz & Co. (*q.v.*). Disc sizes ranged from 7in (17.5cm) to 20½in (52cm). The rarely seen music boxes were made in both horizontal and upright models.

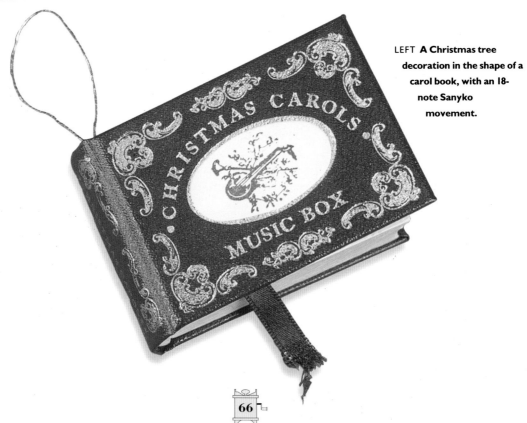

LEFT **A Christmas tree decoration in the shape of a carol book, with an 18-note Sanyko movement.**

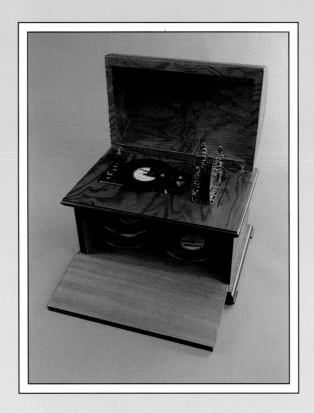

MUSIC BOX MANUFACTURERS

CHAPTER 8

The following are just a few of the many companies in Europe and the United States making both cylinder and disc music boxes. Many manufacturers of cylinder music boxes did not stamp the movements to identify them, and most may only be identified by the information printed on the tune sheets. Where known, the dates during which a company was manufacturing music boxes have been included after the town or city in which the company was based.

ABRAHAMS, BARNETT HENRY
Sainte-Croix, Switzerland, *c.* 1857–*c.* 1900
Maker of cheap, popular cylinder movements, many with bells. Later made the disc music boxes Britannia and Imperial. The cylinder-playing Victoria, an upright, cabinet-type of box, had three bells and was made with and without a coin mechanism. Trademarks: *B.H.A.*; lion with a globe inside a sunburst.

ALIBERT, FRANÇOIS
Paris, France, 1880–*c.* 90
Maker of good quality cylinder boxes, most with small movements. Also repaired movements from other manufacturers.

LEFT **This domed chest is for a 4½in (11cm) modern Thorens disc player. The movement is mounted in the upper, domed section. The chest is finished with an Italian design, and this adds a great deal to the value of the item.**

ALLARD & SANDOZ
Geneva, Switzerland, 1880
Made cylinder music boxes.
Trademark: seated eagle below *Trade Mark* and *Marque de Fabrique* printed on tune sheet.

ALLIEZ & BERGUER
Geneva, Switzerland, 1820–40
Made cylinder music boxes.

AMERICAN MUSIC BOX CO.
Hoboken, New Jersey, USA
Manufactured the Monarch and Triumph disc music boxes.

AUBERT, A.
Switzerland, *c.*1900; moved to London in 1907
Manufacturer and repairer of cylinder boxes.
Trademark: name stamped on comb.

AUBERT, DANIEL
Sainte-Croix, Switzerland, 1879
Made cylinder music boxes. In 1881 patented a device for long-playing musical movements for use with 8-day clocks.

AUBERT FILS
Geneva, Switzerland
Manufacturer of musical snuff-boxes.
Trademark: name stamped on comb.

AUBERT, MOISE
Le Lieu, Vallée de Joux, Switzerland
Early 19th-century makers of cylinder music boxes.

AUBERT & SONS
Sainte-Croix, Switzerland, *c.*1881
Made good quality cylinder music boxes.

BAKER, GEORGE & CO.
Geneva, Switzerland, *c.*1870
Known for good quality, large cylinder boxes. The company made an improved revolver box with three interchangeable cylinders. Later became Baker-Troll & Co.
Trademark: name printed on tune sheet.

BAKER-TROLL & CO.
Geneva, Switzerland, *c.*1880
The partnership of George Baker and Samuel Troll (*qq.v.*) made good quality music boxes, including many with interchangeable cylinders.
Trademark: stylized *BTB* (with first B reversed) stamped on top of cock and tooled into inner lid strap.

BALL, BEAVON & CO.
London, England
Acted as agents for Swiss manufacturers.

Trademark: *BB&C* printed on tune sheet.

BARNETT, SAMUEL & CO.
London, England, 1832
Agent and wholesaler.
Trademark: triangle (musical instrument) with striker below *Trade Mark* and above *Dulcet* printed on tune sheet.

BENDON, GEORGE & CO.
Sainte-Croix, Switzerland; also Holborn, London, England
Probably an agent and importer, although claimed to manufacture cylinder boxes at a factory in Switzerland.
Trademark: large coat of arms with the British lion and unicorn.

BERENS, BLUMBERG & CIE
Geneva, Switzerland, and London, England
Made good quality cylinder music boxes and also imported Lecoultre boxes and acted as agents for many Swiss manufacturers. Their mark is sometimes difficult to distinguish from that of Ball, Beavon & Co. (*q.v.*).
Trademark: *BBC LB* in a rectangle stamped into comb. Cursive *BB&Cie* stamped into top left of bedplate.

LEFT **A beautiful, lacquered box with a high-gloss finish from Sorrento in Italy. The design is made of pieces of contrasting wood inlaid using marquetry. The central instruments are surrounded by a floral design and the box has wooden feet mounted at each corner.**

BILLON-HALLER, JEAN

Geneva, Switzerland, *c.*1880

Made cylinder music boxes.

Trademark: butterfly with letter *J* and *B* in each wing below *Trade Mark* printed on tune sheet.

BONTEM(P)S

Paris, France, 1840

Founded by Blaise Bontems; he was succeeded by his sons Charles and Alfred and by his grandson Lucien. A specialist automata maker, the company was especially known for its fine mechanical singing birds and tableaux.

Trademark: *Bontems Paris Bte SGDG* in an oval stamped into brass plates.

BORDIER, A.

Geneva, Switzerland, *c.*1785

Made good quality movements for cylinder music boxes.

BORDIER FRÈRES

Geneva, Switzerland, 1815–30

Made small movements with sectional and one-piece combs for cylinder music boxes.

BORDIER, M.

Geneva, Switzerland, 1815–30

Made small, good quality music boxes.

Trademark: name stamped on the bedplate or comb.

BORNAND, ADRIAN

New York, USA

Formed Bornand Musical Box Co., Pelham New York

BORTMANN, G. & KELIER, A.

Leipzig, Germany, *c.*1985–*c.*1901

Made the Sirion, a rare type of disc music box.

BREMOND B. A.

Geneva, Switzerland, *c.*1860

Manufactured cylinder boxes.

LEFT **This Thorens 4½in (11cm) disc player is mounted in the box shown on page 68.** The lid is opened to reveal the shining mechanism and a Dune disc in position. The discs are stored on a mounting fixed to the inside of the lid.

Trademarks: *BAB* (the first *B* reversed) in a circle or under a lyre stamped into top of cock or printed on tune sheet. The handle of the winding lever is often stamped with the serial number.

BRUGER & STRAUB

High Holborn, London, England

Importers of music boxes.

Trademark: triangle and striker.

CONCHON, F., & CIE

Geneva, Switzerland, *c.*1874–98

Many of the movements made by this company were of the more unusual types such as the harpe éolienne or the sublime harmonie. Made many good quality cylinder boxes, including some with three or four combs.

Trademarks: *Marque de Fabrique Star Works* in a circle around a star or an oval around a star printed on tune sheet. Two ovals, one containing intertwined *FC* or *FCL*, the other a lyre, separated by three dots stamped into top of cock.

CUENDET, JOHN E.

L'Auberson, Switzerland, *c.*1870–1991

The family made good quality music boxes from 1870. The company John

Cuendet et Ed. was registered at L'Auberson in 1895. In 1991 the company was bought by Reuge SA (*q.v.*).

Trademark: *JC* on either side of a foul anchor in a shield printed on tune sheet.

DAWKINS, THOMAS & CO.

Geneva, Switzerland, 1880–1914

The comb screw washers were sometimes made in the form of brass rosettes, and there was sometimes a knurled flange at the end of the cylinder.

Trademark: sphinx printed on tune sheet or stamped on governor bracket.

DUCOMMUN-GIROD, F. W.

Geneva, Switzerland, 1840–60

Manufactured cylinder boxes, many characterized by trills in the upper register.

Trademark: sunburst containing a face; the name sometimes stamped on bedplate or comb.

EHRLICH, PAUL, & CO. (FABRIK LEIPZIGER MUSIKWERKE)

Leipzig, Germany, *c.*1893

Manufactured the disc music boxes known as Gloria and Monopol.

L'EPÉE
Saint-Suzanne, Doubs, France,
1798–1914
Introduced the child's manivelle, a
popular, hand-turned, small cylinder
movement. Although this company
was a well-known maker of music
boxes in its own right, it also
manufactured boxes for Thibouville-
Lamy & Co. (q.v.).
Trademark: name sometimes appeared
on tune sheet though most are not
marked.

FALCONNET & REYMOND
Geneva, Switzerland, c.1830
Known for making very fine overture
boxes.
Trademark: name stamped on comb or
bedplate.

GENOUX, AMI
Trademark: dagger stamped on brass
components.

GRANGER, JEAN FRANÇOIS
Geneva, Switzerland
See Lecoultre & Granger

GROSZ, B., & CO. (TROUBADOUR-MUSIKWERKE)
Leipzig, Germany
Made the rare Troubadour disc
music box.

HARMONIA SA
L'Auberson, Sainte-Croix, Switzerland
Manufactured the Harmonia disc
music box.

HELBIG, OTTO, & POLIKEIT
Made disc music boxes.

HELLER, J. H.
Berne, Switzerland, c.1870
Known for producing large, good
quality music boxes.
Trademark: name printed on tune
sheet.

HENRIOT
Geneva, Switzerland, c.1870
Trademark: name stamped on
bedplate.

HERMANN, HEINRICH
Trademark: two children and anchor
printed on discs for Celeste.

HOLZWEISSIG, ERNST, UND NACHFOLGER
Major Leipzig distributor.
Trademark: entwined cursive *EH*
above *L* printed on tune sheets.

JACOT, CHARLES HENRY, & CO.
New York, USA
Manufactured music boxes and
invented the Jacot Safety Check, a
device that prevented the cylinder
movements from having an accidental
run.

JUNGHANSSCHE UHRENFABRIK
Württemberg, Germany
Made the Junghans disc music box,
and are known also to have produced
musical clocks with a 4½in (11cm)
disc.
Trademark: *J* within a star stamped on
the disc.

JUNOD, ALFRED
Sainte-Croix, Switzerland, c.1887
A maker of good quality cylinder
boxes, and the inventer of the duplex.

JUNOD, SOCIÉTÉ
Association of Alfred Junod (q.v.),
Jules Jaccard and Paul Calame
Jaccard for the design and
manufacture of music boxes.
Trademarks: shield stamped on
accessories with patent numbers. *JCd*
stamped into bedplate.

KALLIOPE MUSIKWERKE
Leipzig, Germany 1895–1910
Known for the pleasant sound
achieved through the entire range of
its music boxes, the company used
many of its items in novelties such as
gambling machines, automata and
Christmas tree stands. It produced the
Kalliope disc box and a Panorama
series of models featuring a moving
horse race while the music plays.

ABOVE **This contemporary (c.1980)
crystal box has a three-tune, 50-note
(3/50) movement by Reuge, which plays
"Rhapsody in Blue" in three parts. The
crystal sides and top are mounted on a
wood base that has dolphin feet. The
movement is activated by a knob and
lever assembly, which is located at the
front left-hand corner.**

KOMET MUSIKWERKE
Germany, 1895–1902
Manufactured the Komet disc music box.

LANGDORFF & FILS
Geneva, Switzerland, 1850–70
Manufactured good quality cylinder boxes, including some overture mechanisms.
Trademark: harp stamped into top of cock and printed on tune sheet. Carillon keyboard printed on tune sheet.

LECOULTRE, C.
Sainte-Croix, Switzerland
Trademark: name printed on tune sheet.

LECOULTRE, DAVID
Le Brassus, Switzerland, 1810–50
Some boxes have teeth with square tips and a steel bedplate.
Trademark: name printed on distinctive tune sheet.

LECOULTRE, FRANÇOIS-CHARLES
Geneva, Switzerland
The brother of David Lecoultre (q.v.).

LECOULTRE FRÈRES
Geneva, Switzerland, c.1860
Trademark: *LF Gve* or *LB* in a lozenge stamped on the comb.

LECOULTRE, HENRI JOSEPH
Geneva, Switzerland, 1822–56
The leading maker of cylinder music boxes in Geneva. The first maker of boxes with interchangeable cylinders and cylinders that could be fitted to other, similar boxes. Was in partnership with Jean François Granger.

LECOULTRE & GRANGER
Geneva, Switzerland, 1840–44
Company formed by the partnership between Henri Lecoultre and Jean François Granger. Made rare single-comb forte-piano cylinder boxes.

LOCHMANN, PAUL
Zeulenroda, Germany, c.1885
In 1885–6 patented the first music box to play interchangeable tune sheets and made the first disc music box, the Symphonion, in 1885. Also manufactured the Eroica and Lochmann-Original disc music boxes. The company also made a disc

orchestrion, which played string, tubular bells, drum and triangle. Named the Original Konzert Piano, it was weight driven.

LOCHMANNSCHER MUSIKWERKE AKTIENGESELLSCHAFT
Gohlis, Leipzig
The factory at which Paul Lochmann (q.v.) manufactured the Symphonion.

LUDWIG & WILD
Leipzig, Germany
Made the Orpheus disc box from 1897.
Trademark: cursive *Orpheus* printed on discs.

MALIGNON, ALPHONSE
Geneva, Switzerland, c.1835
An early maker of cylinder boxes, including the rare single-comb forte-piano model. Also made overture boxes.

MAYLAN, PHILIPPE-SAMUEL
Le Brassus and Geneva, Switzerland, c.1805
The first maker of musical watches with steel teeth and a disc.
Trademark: *PM* stamped on the movement.

BELOW AND RIGHT **This large jewelry case with inlaid decorations dates from the early 1990s. The case houses an 18-note Reuge movement** **that is activated when the lid is opened. The type of box is also available with 36- and 72-note movements.**

LEFT This inlaid case was made in the mid-1980s in Sorrento, Italy. The case houses a three-tune, 72-note (3/72) Reuge movement, and the winding key is located under the case, which has wooden feet. The floral pattern on the top is inlaid against a natural background, and is accented by the polished lacquer finish. The lid design is enhanced by the fine inlaid borders and light-finished countered edge.

MELODIES SA

L'Auberson, Sainte-Croix
Small factory run by Jean Paul Thorens producing musical movements under the tradename Melodies.

MERMOD FRÈRES

Sainte-Croix, Switzerland, 1815–89
This leading European maker, with a reputation for producing an excellent style of tune arrangements, produced a variety of music boxes, including coin-operated units. Boxes are known for their bright, vibrant sound. Disc music boxes were marketed as Empress, Mira and Stella, and the company also produced cylinder boxes.
Trademark: S twined around a cross printed on tune sheet. MF 1816 around S twined around a cross in a shield stamped on accessories. S twined around a cross in a five-pointed star above Swiss printed design on discs for the Stella.

METERT, HENRY

Geneva, Switzerland, later London, England, c.1903
Trademarks: name or piano keyboard standing on three lyre-shaped legs stamped on bedplate.

MOJON, MANGER & CO.

London, England, and Geneva, Switzerland, c.1880
Makers of large cylinder music boxes, including many interchangeable cylinders and large fixed-cylinder mechanisms. Some boxes had dancing dolls or bells and drums. They also made coin-operated cylinder boxes, and long-playing mechanisms that played for up to 150 minutes on one winding.
Trademarks: MM & Cie in an oval within an ornate shield above Garantie Officielle in a banner printed on tune sheets. MMC stamped on governor bracket.

MOULINIE AÎNÉ

Geneva, Switzerland, c.1829
Made high quality overture music boxes.
Trademark: name stamped on bedplate.

NEUMANN, A. W.

Gohlis, Leipzig, Germany, 1893–4
Made Euterpephon disc music boxes.
Trademark: Euterpephon in a banner and a lyre stamped on center-drive discs.

NICOLE, FRANÇOIS

Geneva, Switzerland, 1776–1849
Trademarks: Francs Nicole stamped on comb of earlier boxes. Later boxes stamped F. Nicole on comb and bedplate.

NICOLE FRÈRES

Geneva, Switzerland, later London, England, 1815–1906
The most famous name in cylinder music boxes from the early years of their development and production. The company is credited with the introduction of the "forte-piano" movement, and is known for excellent quality and for having produced more than 40,000 music boxes by 1880. The movements and tune sheets are marked with their name. Unless it is made of cast iron, the name Nicole Frères is stamped on the left back of the bedplate and is also found on the comb. The company's boxes may be dated fairly accurately, and readers are referred to the books by David Tallis and John E. T. Clarke listed in Further Reading.
Trademarks: globe in square between the words Trademark, registered by Charles Eugène Brun 2 August 1882 and printed on tune sheets.

OLBRICH, A.
Vienna, Austria
Makers of good quality musical
movements, which are often found in
clocks.
Trademark: name stamped on bedplate
and on bass teeth on right-hand side of
the comb.

OTTO, F. G. & SONS
Jersey City, New Jersey, USA, 1895
The company produced three lines of
disc players – the Capital Cuff Box,
the Criterion, and the Olympia.

PAILLAIRD, AMÉDÉE
Sainte-Croix, Switzerland, c.1860
Designed and patented a changeable
cylinder box and in 1870 patented a
famous (though rare) revolver, multi-
cylinder music box. He also patented
an interchangeable cylinder box in
which the cylinders could be changed
from box to box.

PAILLARD, CHARLES
Sainte-Croix, Switzerland, c.1850
One of the largest family businesses to
be involved in the making of music
boxes and was a dominant supplier in
Europe. Paillard took over Thorens
(q.v.) after World War II, but was itself
taken over by the Austrian company
Eumig. Paillard ceased manufacturing
music boxes in 1894, but it still makes
Bolex ciné cameras and Hermes
typewriters.
Trademarks: *CP&C* separated by
vertical and horizontal line stamped on
top of cock. Foul anchor stamped into
top of cock.

PAILLARD, ERNEST
Sainte-Croix, Switzerland
In conjunction with his brother-in-law
Eugene Thorens, Paillard devised a
method of stamping gears and wheels.

This was a major step towards the
mass-production of movements.

PAILLARD, VAUCHER, FILS
Trademark: *PVF* in oblong stamped on
comb, control lever mount or governor
bracket or printed on tune sheet; also
engraved on top of accessory zither
attachment.

PERFECTION MUSIC BOX CO.
Jersey City, New Jersey, USA
1898–1901
Manufactured the Perfection disc
music box.

PIETSCHMANN, & SON
Berlin, Germany, *fl.* 1895
Trademark: two spoked wheels above
Trade Mark in cartouche printed on
discs of Celesta disc machine.

PIGUET & MEYLAN
Trademark: *P&M* above number
stamped into music disc. Four small
horseshoe shapes above *80* stamped
on music disc.

POLYPHON MUSIKWERKE
Leipzig, Germany, c.1891–1914
Made the Polyphon range of disc
music boxes. See also Chapter 2.

ABOVE **The same box as shown on page
72 with the lid opened to show the
movement and tune sheet.**

RAYMOND, HENRI FRANÇOIS
Geneva, Switzerland, c.1827–63
Known also as Raymond Nicole. Made
fine quality cylinder music boxes.
Trademark: signed *Raymond-nicole* or
Reymond-Nicole on the comb.

REGINA MUSIC BOX CO.
Rahway, New Jersey, USA, 1892–
1919
Manufacturers of Regina disc music
boxes. See also Chapter 2.

REUGE SA
Sainte-Croix, Switzerland, 1886
Still in existence, this company is
known for producing fine music boxes.
In recent years it has become the
leading maker in Europe, and it
continues to make an excellent range
of mechanical movements. The
company employs 170 people and
manufactures almost all its own parts.
In 1985 Reuge bought Melodies SA
(q.v.) of L'Auberson, manufacturers of
disc and cylinder-type movements
which were sold under the name
Thorens (q.v.), which was well known
in the United States. In 1986 Reuge
bought Lador SA, of Sainte-Croix,
manufacturers of 18-note low-end
musical movements. Until 1988 Reuge
was a family-owned company, but it
was bought out and has since
successfully concentrated selling
efforts in the Far East and Europe,
although marketing to the United
States is now underway. In 1991
Reuge bought Cuendet SA (q.v.) of
L'Auberson, a company that had
specialized in movements for cuckoo-
clocks.
Trademarks: music boxes are marked
Reuge Music. Musical movements up
to 72-note size marked *Romance*.

RIGHT **An 18-note Sankyo movement plays the tune in this 1990s musical kaleidoscope, and the same movement turns the circular disc with its stained-glass and "jewels". You can see a changing array of colors and shapes when you look through the barrel.**

RICHTER, FRIEDRICH ADOLF, & CO.

Rudolstadt, Germany, 1876
Made the Imperator disc music box
and the Libellion.

RIVENC, AMI

Trademark: left-facing winged lion
stamped into top of cock. Reverse
image printed on tune sheet.

ROCHAT FRÈRES

Geneva, Switzerland, 1810–25

ABOVE **A Thorens 11in (28cm) disc player in a European-style case. The winding handle is located on the left-hand side of the case.**

Known for fine singing birds in snuff-boxes, cages, parasol handles, etc.
Trademark: *FR* in a diamond or,
occasionally, a circle or oval stamped
into brass work.

RZEBITSCHEK, FRANTIZEK

Josefov, later Prague, Czechoslovakia
Won first prize for music boxes at the
Great Exhibition in London in 1851.
Also made small movements for use in
clocks, sewing baskets, pictures, and
other domestic items. The combs
sometimes had the bass teeth located
on the right-hand side. The company
was taken over by Gustave,
Frantizek's son, in 1870.
Trademark: name (sometimes
rendered *Rebicek*) stamped on
bedplate.

SALLAZ & OBOUSSIER

Sainte-Croix, Switzerland, c.1840–50
Made good quality cylinder boxes. The
inner glass lid was hinged on the
upper back edge.
Trademark: name printed on tune
sheet.

SANKYO SEIKI MFG. CO., LTD.

Minato-ku, Tokyo, Japan, 1946
In 1948 Sankyo was the first Japanese
company to begin research into

musical movements, and it soon
became dominant in the production of
smaller movements that had up to 18
notes. By 1985 the company was
producing the Orpheus, a 50-note
music box. It also produces a novelty
movement with bells with bee striker
hammers and a more traditional
movement with a 30-note range.

SCHRÄMLI & TSCHUDIN (SUN MUSIC BOX MANUFACTURING CO.)

Geneva, Switzerland, c.1903
Makers of the Sun disc music box,
examples of which are not known to
have survived.

SILBER & FLEMING

Trademark: *AMS* in a bow printed on
tune sheets.

SOCIÉTÉ ANONYME

Geneva, Switzerland
Manufactured the disc music boxes
known as the Gloria and the Polymnia.

SYMPHONIONFABRIK CO.

Gohlis, Leipzig, Germany, 1885–1902

ABOVE **A contemporary manivelle or child's hand-cranked music box made by Thorens around 1975. The piece has a single-tune, 18-note cylinder movement that plays when the handle is turned. Interestingly, the tune is played whether the handle is turned backwards or forwards.**

Manufactured the Symphonion disc music box. See also Chapter 2.

TANNHÄUSER MUSIKWERKE
Lindenau, Leipzig, Germany, 1898–1900
Manufactured the very rare Tannhäuser disc music box.

THIBOUVILLE-LAMY, JEROME, & CO.
Geneva, Switzerland, *c.*1850
Manufacturer of cylinder boxes. The bedplates were usually made of copper-plated gun-metal and mounted in the case from the bottom. The winding lever usually has a wooden handle, and the partition that holds the control levers is screwed together so that the screw heads are visible.
Trademark: lyre above *J.T.L.* printed on tune sheets, mostly L'Epée boxes.

THORENS, HERMANN
Sainte-Croix, Switzerland, 1881–1985
Produced musical movements and music boxes until 1985, when it was bought by Reuge SA (*q.v.*). Known for its modern cylinder movements, which are found in many popular collectors' items, such as wooden boxes with revolving tops. The revolving portion often had wooden, hand-carved figures – e.g., Anri – and the base usually had a 28-note movement. The company's movements are also found mounted in a wide range of cases, ranging from simple, well-finished plain boxes to boxes with ornately decorated wooden inlay designs. The disc music boxes were sold under the names Edelweiss and Helvetia. The company was bought by Paillard (*q.v.*) after World War II, and Jean Paul Thorens opened a factory in L'Auberson to produce movements under the tradename Melodies (*q.v.*).
Trademark: anchor cast into bedplate of Edelweiss disc machine.

ULLMANN, CHARLES & J.
L'Auberson, Switzerland, 1870–90
Maker of cylinder music boxes. The tune sheets are highly colored.
Trademarks: *Qualité Excelsior* in a circle around a triangle stamped into comb or top of cock. *ChU* in a triangle stamped into bedplate; also found cast into underside of bedplate. Winged lion and shield containing *ChU* below *Qualité Excelsior* and above *Superextra*.

WEILL & HARBURG
Trademark: stylized angular *W&H* printed on tune sheets.

WEISSBACH & CO.
Trademark: man playing a horn above *Schutzmark* printed on discs for Komet.

WILLENBACHER & RZEBITSCHEK
Prague, Czechoslovakia
The bass teeth were located on the right-hand side of the comb. See also Rzebitschek.
Trademark: name stamped on bedplate.

WOOG, ADOLPHE
Early importer of L'Epée.
Trademark: *AW* in an oval stamped into top left of bedplate. *Trade Mark* and *AW* around anchor above *Registered* within shield; registered on 8 December 1876 and printed on tune sheets. Woman holding a shield with *AW* around anchor within shield below *Trade Mark* and above *Registered*.

WOOG, SAMUEL
Early importer of L'Epée.
Trademarks: *SW* in an oval stamped into top left of bedplate.

ZIMMERMANN, JULIUS H. (ADLER MUSIKWERKE)
Gohlis, Leipzig, Germany, 1896
Took over the Adler line of disc music boxes in 1900 and changed the name to Fortuna.
Trademark: eagle in flight in front of sunburst below *Shutzmarke* with *Patented* in a banner and *Trade Mark* below.

ZUMSTEQ, HEINRICH
Kulm, Aarqua, Germany, *c.*1885
Designed a system of gears that increased the playing time of music boxes.

LEFT **This distressed pine case (by Elpha Marketing) for a 4½in (11cm) Thorens disc player was made in the 1970s. The interior of the box holds the movement and has a partitioned area for storing the discs.**

SOCIETIES

If you are interested in music boxes you will want to take every opportunity to see and hear different types. One of the ways of enjoying music boxes is to share the pleasure with the people who own them; another way is to visit museums and public collections where they can be seen and, on occasion, heard. It can be difficult to locate antique music boxes, and some international collections are listed in the next section, Collections to Visit.

However, if you are interested in seeing as wide a range of styles of music boxes as possible you will probably find it worth while joining the Musical Box Society International (MBSI). The Society has more than 2,500 members in the United States and 18 other countries, ranging from Australia to Japan to Europe. There are also other, smaller national societies dedicated to music boxes, including those in Britain, France and Germany. No one who is seriously interested in the subject should fail to join one or more of these societies.

The MBSI also publishes a directory of members and museums, and this information is a valuable source of information about music boxes that may be seen and enjoyed. The directory lists members and dealers, as well as indicating the items and range of their interest and collections. Please note that if you do decide to join the MBSI and wish to take advantage of the information contained in the directory by visiting any of the dealers or collectors listed therein, you should always write or at least telephone in advance of your visit to agree a mutually convenient time.

THE MUSICAL BOX SOCIETY INTERNATIONAL
PO Box 205
Route 3
Morgantown
IN 46160

THE MUSICAL BOX SOCIETY OF GREAT BRITAIN
The Willows
102 High Street
Landbeach
Cambridge
CB4 4DT

The MBSI has two museums – in Cleveland, Ohio, and in Norwalk, Connecticut – and their addresses are given in Collections to Visit.

DEALERS, RESTORERS, SUPPLIERS, AND MANUFACTURERS

The annual directory of the Musical Box Society International contains details of dealers, restorers, suppliers and manufacturers.

For a catalog of music box restoration parts and supplies contact: Nancy Fratti, Panchronia Antiquities, PO Box, Route 4, Whitehall, NY 128877, USA. A charge is made for supplying this catalog.

FURTHER READING

BOWERS, Q. David, *Encyclopedia of Automatic Musical Instruments*, The Vestal Press Ltd., Vestal, New York 13850, 1972

BULLEID, H(enry) A(nthony) V(aughan), *Cylinder Musical Box Design and Repair*, Almar Press, Binghampton, New York, 1987

CHAPUIS, Alfred, *Histoire de la Boîte à Musique et de la Musique Mécanique*, Editions Scriptar, Lausanne, Switzerland, 1955 (translated as *History of the Musical Box and of Mechanical Music* by Joseph E. Roesch)

CLARKE, John E. T., *Musical Boxes*, George Allen & Unwin Ltd., London and Boston, 1961

ORD-HUME, Arthur W. J. G., *Musical Box: A History and Collector's Guide*, George Allen & Unwin Ltd., London and Boston, 1980

ORD-HUME, Arthur W. J. G., *Restoring Musical Boxes*, George Allen & Unwin Ltd., London and Boston, 1980

TALLIS, David, *Musical Boxes: A Guide for Collectors*, Stein & Day, New York, New York, 1971

WEBB, Graham, *The Cylinder Musical Box Handbook*, Faber & Faber, London, 1968; The Vestal Press Ltd., Vestal, New York 13850, 1984

WEBB, Graham, *The Disc Musical Box Handbook*, Faber & Faber, London 1971; The Vestal Press Ltd., Vestal, New York 13850, 1986

YOUNG, David R., *How Old is my Music Box?*, Rochester, New York

COLLECTIONS TO VISIT

The following is an, inevitably, abbreviated list of museums and collections around the world. For details of items shown, opening hours, and specific addresses you are advised to contact the collection itself if you are in the area.

AUSTRALIA
Powerhouse, Ultimo, Sydney, New South Wales

AUSTRIA
Technische Museum für Industrie und Gewerbe, Vienna
The Vienna Clock Museum, Vienna

BELGIUM
Museum of Instruments of the Royal Conservatory of Music, Brussels
Museum of the Belfrye, Ghent
Museum van Muziekdoos Tot Grammofoon, St Niklaas

CANADA
Eberdt Museum of Communications History, Quebec
National Museum of Science and Technology, Sutton, Ottawa, Ontario

CZECH REPUBLIC
Museum of Decorative Arts, Prague

FINLAND
Mekaanisen Musiikin Museo, Varkaus

FRANCE
Decamps, Maison, Paris
Goujon, Marcel (private collection), Giraumont-Tourotte
Manufacture de Limonaires, Vienne, Isère
Marchal, Claude P. (private collection), Paris
Musée Arturo Lopez, Neuilly-sur-Seine, Hauts-de-Seine
Musée de l'Automate, Souillac, Lot
Musée de Château, Montbeliard, Belfort, Doubs
Musée de la Musique Mécanique, Combrit
Musée des Musiques Mécaniques, Les Gets
Musée du Phonographe et de la Musique Mécanique, Saint-Maximin-La-Sainte-Baume, Var
Musée National des Techniques, Paris

GERMANY
Auto und Technik Museum, Sinsheim, Kraichgau, Baden-Württemberg
Deutsches Museum, München (Munich), Bavaria
Deutsches Uhrenmuseum Furtwangen, Furtwangen, Baden-Württemberg
Klimperkasten, Köln (Cologne), Rhine-Westphalia
Mechanisches Musik-Museum, Landenburg
Museum für Verkehr und Technik Braunschweig, Berlin 61
Museum Mechanischer Musikinstrumenten, Bruchsal, Baden-Württemberg
Musikinstrumenten-Museum des Staatlichen Instituts für Musikforschung, Berlin 30
Musik Museum Burg Linz/Rhine, Rheinland-Pfalz (Rhineland Palatinate)
Musik Museum, Monschau
Phonomuseum, Georgen, Schwarzwald-Bar-Kris
Regional Gesichte und Orgelbau Elztalmuseum, Waldkirch
Sammlung von Spieldosen und Mechanischer Musikinstrumentem, Steinbreite
Schuhkechts Musikwissenschaftliches Museum, Hanover, Lower Saxony
Schwarzald-Museum, Tribert, Baden-Württemberg
Siegfrieds Mechanisches Musikkabinett, Ruedesheim, Hessen
Stadtsmuseum-Musikinstrumenten-museum, München (Munich), Bavaria
Wuppertaler Uhrenmuseum, Wuppertal-Elberfeld, Rhine-Westphalia

ITALY
Museo di Strumenti Musicali Meccanici, Savio, Ravenna

JAPAN
Hall of Halls, Kitakoma-Gun, Yamanishi-Ken
Japanese Antique Clock Museum, Kamakura, Kanazawa

MONACO
Musée National de Monaco, Monte Carlo

NETHERLANDS
Draaiorgelmuseum, Assen, Drenthe
Gaviolizaal, Helmond, Brabant
Kijk en Luister Museum, Bennekom
National Museum ("From Musical Clock to Street Organ"), Utrecht
Stichting Netherlands Piano Museum, Amsterdam
Stichting Stadorgel Haarlem ("Het Kunkels Orgel"), Haarlem

NORWAY
Norsk Teknisk Museum, Oslo
Ringve Museum, Trondheim

SWITZERLAND

Breschbuhl, famille de H. (private collection), Steffisburg, Berne

C.I.M.A. (International Centre of Mechanical Art)

Fredy's Mechanisches Musikmuseum, Neuchâtel

L'Homme et le Temps, La Chaux-de-Fonds, Neuchâtel

Marchal, Claude P. (private collection), Bullet, Vaud

Musée Baud, L'Auberson, Vaud

Musée d'Art et d'Histoire, Sainte-Croix

Musée de l'Horlogerie du Château des Monts-Le Locle, Le Locle, Neuchâtel

Musée de l'Horlogerie et de l'Emaillerie, Geneva

Musée International de l'Horlogerie Lichtenstein, St Gallen

Musikautomaten Museum, Sion, Valais

Retonio's Mechanisches Musik und Zaubermuseum, Appenzell, St Gallen

UNITED KINGDOM

CHESHIRE

Stapeley Yesteryear Collection, Nantwich

CORNWALL

Paul Corin Music Museum, Liskeard

DURHAM

The Bowes Museum, Barnard Castle

GLOUCESTERSHIRE

Museum of Mechanical Musical Instruments and Clocks, Northleach

HERTFORDSHIRE

St Albans Organ Museum, Camp Road, St Albans

LONDON

British Museum, Great Russell Street, Westminster

Victoria & Albert Museum, Cromwell Road, South Kensington

MIDDLESEX

Musical Museum, Brentford

NORFOLK

The Thursford Collection, Fakenham

NORTHAMPTONSHIRE

Turner's Musical Merry-Go-Round, Wooton, Northampton

OXFORD

Pitt Rivers Museum, South Parks Road

SOUTH GLAMORGAN

National Museum of Wales, Cathays Park, Cardiff

SUFFOLK

Mechanical Music Museum Trust, Cotton, Stowmarket

WARWICKSHIRE

The Napton Museum of Mechanical Music, Napton-on-the-Hill, near Rugby

WEST MIDLANDS

Birmingham Museum and Art Gallery, Chamberlain Square, Birmingham

Birmingham Museum of Science and Industry, Newhall Street, Birmingham

WEST SUSSEX

Mechanical Music and Doll Collection, Chichester

YORKSHIRE

Museum of Automata, York

Penny Arcadia, Pocklington, York

Top Farm, West Hardwick, near Wakefield

UNITED STATES

ARIZONA

Arizona Historical Society, Tucson

ARKANSAS

Miles Musical Museum, Eureka Springs

CALIFORNIA

Calico Ghost Town, Calico

Disneyland, Anaheim

Kearney Mansion Museum, Fresno

Knott's Berry Farm and Ghost Town, Buena Park

Merle Norman Cosmetics Classic Beauty Collection, Sylmar

Musée Mécanique, San Francisco

Sam's Town, Shingle Springs

Scotty's Castle (National Park Service), Death Valley National Monument, Death Valley

COLORADO

Pikes Peak Ghost Town, Colorado Springs

Shull Pianos and Antiques, Inc., Arriba

CONNECTICUT

The American Museum of Mechanical Music, East Hampton

Johnson Victrola Museum, Delaware, Dover

Museum of the Musical Box Society International, The Lockwood-Mathews Mansion Museum, 295 West Avenue, Norwalk

FLORIDA

Bell's Cars and Music of Yesterday, Sarasota

Disney World, Lake Buena Vista

Edison Winter Home and Museum, Fort Meyers

Elliott Museum, Stuart

Jacksonville Museum of Arts and Science, Jacksonville

Lightner Museum, St Augustine

Old South Bar, Clewiston

St Petersburg Historical Museum, St Petersburg

Staie, Ione and Harold, Intercession City

GEORGIA

Antique Auto and Music Museum, Stone Mountain

IDAHO

Magnum's Musical Arcade, Blackfoot

ILLINOIS

Aurora Historical Museum, Aurora

Museum of Science and Industry, Chicago

Pedals, Pumpers, and Rolls, Batavia

Ringer and Son Hall of Fine Musical
  Arts and Performances, Berlin

Seven Acres Antique Village and
  Museum, Union

The Time Museum, Rockford

INDIANA

Julia Meek Garr Wayne County,
  Indiana Historical Museum,
  Richmond

La Porte County Historical Museum,
  La Porte

Midwest Phonograph Museum,
  Martinsville

IOWA

Billy Clock Exhibit, Spillville

Plymouth County Historical Museum,
  Le Mars

KANSAS

Boot Hill Museum, Inc., Dodge City

Kansas Museum of History, Topeka

MAINE

Musical Wonder House, Wiscasset

Wells Auto Museum, Wells

MARYLAND

Museum and Library of Maryland
  History, Baltimore

MICHIGAN

Henry Ford Museum and Greenfield
  Village, Dearborn

Marquette County Historical Society,
  Marquette

Marvin's Marvelous Mechanical
  Museum, Farmington Hills

Memory Lane Old-Time Arcade,
  Frankenmuth

The Music House, Acme

Stagecoach Stop USA, Onsted

MINNESOTA

The Schubert Clum Kugler Collection,
  St Paul

MONTANA

World Museum of Mining, Butte

NEVADA

Harold's Club Gun Collection and
  Musical Museum, Reno

The Virginia City Museum, Virginia
  City

NEW HAMPSHIRE

Clark's Trading Post, North
  Woodstock

NEW JERSEY

Edison National Historic Site, West
  Orange

Lambert Castle, Patterson

NEW YORK

Buffalo and Erie County Historical
  Society, Buffalo

Empire State Theater and Musical
  Instruments Museum, Syracuse

The F.X. Matt Brewery Tour, Utica

Mahopac Country Store Farm and
  Museum, Baldwin Place

The Musical Museum, Deansboro

O-R-S Music Rolls, Inc., Buffalo

The Strong Museum, Rochester

NORTH DAKOTA

State Historical Society of North
  Dakota, Bismarck

OHIO

George T. Jones House, Granville

Museum of the Musical Box Society
  International, Western Reserve
  Historical Society, 10825 East
  Boulevard, Cleveland

Musique Mechanique Revue,
  Columbus

Palace Theater, Canton

The Wagnalls Memorial, Lithopolis

OKLAHOMA

National Cowboy Hall of Fame and
  Western Heritage Center,

Oklahoma City

PENNSYLVANIA

Antique Music Museum, Franklin

Chester County Historical Society,
  West Chester

The Franklin Institute Science
  Museum, Philadelphia

Hershey Museum, Hershey

Knoebels Amusement Resort,
  Elysburg

Mill Bridge Village, Strasburg

SOUTH DAKOTA

Old West Museum, Hamberlain

Pioneer Auto Museum and Antique
  Town, Murdo

TENNESSEE

Houston Antique Museum,
  Chattanooga

TEXAS

Harris Co. Heritage Society, Houston

Olden Year Musical Museum,
  Duncanville

VERMONT

American Precision Museum,
  Windsor

Shelburne Museum, Shelbourne

VIRGINIA

The Mariner's Museum, Newport
  News

WASHINGTON

Museum of History and Industry,
  Seattle

Washington State Capital Museum,
  Olympia

WISCONSIN

Circus World Museum, Baraboo

Historic Chandler House, Waukesha

House on the Rock, Spring Green

Kalvelage Schloss, Milwaukee

State Historical Museum, Madison

INDEX